THE CANADIAN MANIFESTO

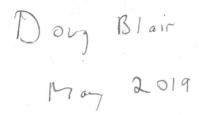

ALSO BY CONRAD BLACK

*Rise to Greatness: A History of Canada
from the Vikings to the Present*

*Flight of the Eagle: A Strategic History
of the United States*

A Matter of Principle

*Franklin Delano Roosevelt:
Champion of Freedom*

THE CANADIAN MANIFESTO

How One Frozen Country Can Save The World

CONRAD BLACK

SUTHERLAND
HOUSE

Sutherland House
416 Moore Ave., Suite 205
Toronto, ON M4G 109

Sutherland House and logo are registered trademarks
of The Sutherland House Inc.

First hardcover edition, May 2019

If you are interested in inviting one of our authors to a live event or
media appearance, please contact publicity@sutherlandhousebooks.com
and visit our website at sutherlandhousebooks.com for more information
about our authors and their schedules.

Manufactured in Canada
Cover designed by Lena Wang
Book composed by Karl Hunt

Library and Archives Canada Cataloguing in Publication
Title: The Canadian manifesto / by Conrad Black
Names: Black, Conrad, author.
Description: Includes bibliographical references.
Identifiers: Canadiana 20190043989 |
ISBN 9781999439552 (hardcover)
Subjects: LCSH: Political planning—Canada. |
LCSH: Canada—Politics and government—21st century. |
LCSH: Political planning.
Classification: LCC JL86.P64 B53 2019 |
DDC 320.60971—dc23

ISBN 978-1-9994395-5-2

CONTENTS

FOREWORD

Jordan Peterson

"Canada is the only bicultural, trans-continental, parliamentary confederation that has ever existed, and as it has
functioned with relatively minor alterations for 151 years, it
is surpassed in seniority of its political institutions, among
countries with more than 20 million people, only by the UK
and the US."

During much of the time I grew up, the national con-
versation in Canada, led mostly by the Toronto media elite,
centered on the importance of distinguishing ourselves conceptually and politically from that monster of myth-making
to our south. It was as if we had to constantly remind ourselves that we were somehow not junior Americans. I think
much of this concern has vanished, as our population has
grown, as we have fostered three truly great cities (Vancouver,
Montreal and Toronto) and some very promising up-and-
comers, and as it has become increasingly obvious, for
not-so-obvious reasons, that we are self-evidently different
from our brothers and sisters in the United States. But we are
still unaware of our own great potential. We suffer from a
national lack of self-confidence, evident in a true paucity of
vision, that drapes itself in the paradoxically self-aggrandizing

cloth of humility and a rather dull sense of our own nice-
ness (the least admirable of virtues). We tend toward guilt,
as well, and upbraid ourselves constantly for our shortcom-
ings—the treatment of native Canadians as the country was
established, the difficulty mediating between the competing
interests of Francophones and Anglophones (and, by exten-
sion, the interests of all the other ethnic groups clamouring
for a voice), and our inability to make the distribution of
wealth equitable at the provincial and, to some degree, individual level. We have paid a price for all this peace-making.
It has made us timid.

In his *Manifesto*, Conrad Black is attempting to change
all that. He starts by re-acquainting us with our history. (Or,
more accurately, by acquainting us with it: Canadians believe
unquestioningly that our peaceful country is dull and has
always been that way, although the latter claim is certainly
not true. There is no shortage of adventure and mystery in
the history of Canada). He points out that we established
our country on the basis not so much of multi-culturalism
but on the principle of reciprocity (avoiding, as the English
did, as Black puts it, "imposing their numerical superiority
on the French") allied with the provision of a great infrastructure—the uniting railway—that was of benefit to all
concerned. This is a highly effective, understated, and prag-
matic approach, uniting amity and productivity, in keeping
with the equally understated broader and fundamentally
Canadian principles of peace, order and good government.
Black details all this in a manner that speaks of fundamental
respect and appropriate gratitude for the great achievements
of our past, without any descent into the mindless patriotism
that merely generates rebellion against its excesses. Those

who founded our country were, by and large (and particularly when compared to political operatives in most other places in the world) careful, practical, decent, and possessed of sufficient scope of vision. I would take that over revolutionary fervor and grandiose utopianism any day, despite its comparative lack of drama. And drama—that is best romanticized in history books than lived through by those subject to its privations, uncertainties and horrors.

We stayed stable and prosperous, comparatively, through the most tumultuous century in human history. That is no mean achievement. Thus, the twentieth century, said by Wilfrid Laurier to belong to Canada, did in fact belong to us in important ways, even though more dramatic events took place in louder and more charismatic countries. We established a country of great peace and prosperity and, as well, one that appears to be improving in stature, strength and possibility. We managed that without the great upheavals that mark states out so markedly on the world stage, and that provide them with an oft-dangerous sense of their own manifest destiny. We contributed in no insignificant manner to the defeat of fascism in the 1930s and 1940s and the defeat of communism during the Cold War years (all detailed with admirable brevity in Black's work). We worked out many of our complex internal contradictions, producing a relatively loose federation that works very well. We are still a country, and even more identifiably so than five decades ago, yet our local institutions retain enough power that local solutions can be generated and tested. With a little vision, perhaps, the 21st century could be more firmly ours, in that our country could be a model for what might constitute the admirable modern state, politically sophisticated, technologically advanced, absent the worship of political leaders that corrupts so may countries (threatening even our great neighbour to the south).

Black's *Manifesto* reminds us who we were and, therefore, who we are. In doing so, he lays the groundwork for us to consider who we might yet become. A peaceful nation, capable of mending its own fences, stable and productive for a time worthy of celebration, with an educated, honest and capable population, not so arrogant as to assume a place of primacy in world affairs, not so timid as to presume ourselves incapable of leadership, not least by example; this is perhaps the best that might be hoped for in this world of vulnerability, complexity, and strife. Maybe we can mature in our self-consciousness. Maybe we can take our place provincially, nationally, and on the world stage with increasing but realistic confidence. Maybe we can continue, in our Canadian way, our process of incremental improvement and cautious improvement and prove the victorious tortoise in a race run by too-impetuous hares.

And maybe that could be abetted by a little more vision of precisely the sort that Black manifests in what is, after all, a *Manifesto*.

INTRODUCTION:
A NEW PURPOSE

Almost all Canadians, all their conscious lives, are disappointed that Canada is under-recognized in the world. Given the strategic facts of its population, economic influence, and longstanding international relationships, it was never going to happen within anyone's lifetime that Canada would emerge as one of the most objectively powerful countries in the world. When Canadian Confederation was approved by the British Parliament in 1867, the broadminded colonial secretary, Lord Carnarvon, said to the House of Lords that a great nation of the future was being created. Wilfrid Laurier said that the twentieth century belongs to Canada, as that century opened. Both statesmen were correct but optimistic in their timing.

Most Canadians who consider the subject at all recognize that Canada is benignly regarded in the world, but is rarely credited with anything beyond being a relatively gentle and democratic society with a good historical record of welcoming diverse immigration, assisting worthy international causes, staying clear of wars yet participating in the great struggles of civilization that have occurred in its time bravely and justly, seeking nothing for itself but the triumph of the principles of human decency and international law. What is missing is distinctiveness and drama. Few Canadians have not been bored with caricatures of red-tunicked mounted police, polar bears, and other reminders of winter, even though Canada's urban winters are less severe than those of Russia or many northern American states.

The absence of drama is an absence of violence, of the clash of heartfelt political and social forces irreconcilable other than by noble and dreadful sacrifice. Even the English have had the dynastic struggles: Cromwell's Civil War, threats of imminent invasion, the Blitz, and the launching of the mighty endeavour of the liberation of Europe in 1944. This is stirring history, especially in the hands of such galvanizing dramatists as Shakespeare and Churchill. And the Americans, though their European origins are almost contemporaneous with ours, had a revolution (however dubious the mythos on which it was based and the lore of its conduct at times) and, only one long life later, a terrible civil war in which 750,000 people perished out of a population only about eighty per cent the size of Canada's today. So vivid are the leading personalities and events of the latter conflict that today there are societies and individuals all over the advanced world whose chief hobby is the study of the Civil War, and the renown of Abraham Lincoln is universal and entirely deserved. Horrible as they were, probably the two most indelible enactments of violence in the modern world were the assassination of President John F. Kennedy in 1963 and the attacks on the World Trade Center Towers in 2001, both preserved on film, and always chilling no matter how often they are replayed.

The absence of violence is far from the whole Canadian story, and no sane person would wish any more of it than we have had in this country, but the task of turning Canada's relative tranquillity into a resonant national asset is difficult. And it is complicated by a chronic underappreciation of the virtues and heroism of our own history, and by the cultural disadvantages of being the third greatest English-speaking culture in the world and the second greatest French-speaking culture, two societies coexisting, sometimes uneasily. Almost all nation-states, from the origin of this method of organization in the sixteenth century until the American Revolution, were discrete cultural units. The English spoke English, the French spoke French, the Chinese, Russians, Swedish, Dutch, Spanish, Portuguese, and others generally defined their territory by their language. Some great cultures were late organizing themselves politically, especially the Germans, Italians, and Japanese. Since its language was taken from the country from which it declared and won its independence, the United States, with the talent for showmanship that has ever attended that nationality, substituted and rose above the confines of language and declared itself a commonwealth for people of all cultures and races, enticing them to depart their "teeming shores" and "breathe free" in America.

The Americans have been overachievers in the creation and pursuit of their national mythos, as in many other spheres. The British had imposed on America a tax their own citizens were already paying to reduce the national debt, which had doubled in the Seven Years' War, largely fought to expel France from North America, and the Americans were the wealthiest of British citizens. Americans had no more freedom at the end of the Revolutionary War than they had had at the beginning of it, although they now had their own government. They had no more civic freedom than did the

British, Swiss, Dutch, and much of Scandinavia. But there was enough truth in their government's claims to be "a new order of the ages" and to be holding up the lamp of human freedom that they are believed by Americans and widely accepted in the world. They became the republican propagandists of freedom, and when Czechs and Poles and others moved to emancipate themselves from the Russians at the end of the twentieth century, they read aloud the works of Lincoln and Jefferson (a slaveholder) to inspire themselves. The United States has always had a winning formula as an immense rich democracy that welcomed ethnic diversity in mass immigration but united in its robust democracy.

When the country rose to be the greatest power on earth and to operate on a scale the world had never imagined possible, its strategic influence and the astuteness of its statesmen assured the triumph of democracy and the free market in the world. America, then, created a fragile mythos, grew into it, and inspired the world with it; in response, the world has largely imitated, with whatever misgivings, the democratic and commercialized life America has propagated. It has been a magnificent spectacle and achievement, and Canadians have had occasion to observe it more closely than others.

Whatever else the United States has accomplished, it has crowded other English-speaking democracies of less dramatic and later genesis and smaller scale, such as Canada and Australia, into a place of comparative ambiguity. The question of Canada's self-identity is compounded by the poor job Canadians have made of understanding and teaching our own history. We can scarcely expect the world to find us interesting if we are not really interested in our own history, development, and unique national achievements.

The purpose of this book is to remind Canadians of the peculiar glories of their past, highlighting some of the accomplishments and strengths that can be built upon, and to suggest a way that Canada, leaving supremacy in arms and wealth to others, can forge a unique and distinguished role for itself in the arts of government by solving some of the developed world's most intractable problems.

PART 1

THE PAST REVEALS
THE FUTURE

Canada is the only bicultural, transcontinental, parliamentary confederation that has ever existed, and as it has functioned with relatively minor alteration for 151 years, it is surpassed in the seniority of its political institutions, among countries with as great a population, only by the United Kingdom and the United States. And the U.K. shed an important province (Ireland) in that time, while just two years before the launch of Canadian Confederation, the United States concluded the terrible war that was necessary to reunite the country, to abolish slavery and to render its claims to championship of the equality of all men remotely believable.

Not one per cent of Canadians would now appreciate that for the country to exist at all as an independent jurisdiction it had to begin as a French colony else it would have been assimilated to the American colonies. It had to become economically self-sufficient under the French, and then pass to the British, as the strategic division between the two leading Western European states was that Britain was supreme at sea while France was supreme within Europe. The French could never determine whether their strategic ambitions incited them to cross the Rhine or the English Channel to increase France's standing in the world. Ultimately France did not succeed in crossing either waterway durably and, across the seas, France had only Britain's leavings, so its occupation of New France (Quebec) could not have endured. In 1763, just thirteen years before the Americans proclaimed their revolt against the British Empire, Canada (chiefly New France) was ceded by France to Britain, avoiding being subsumed into the American colonies and republic.

Samuel de Champlain, who founded New France; Jean Talon, who founded the shipbuilding, iron, textile, and brewing industries that made New France economically self-sufficient, and introduced the one thousand fertile French girls from whom over six million French Canadians and Franco-Americans are now descended; and Louis de Frontenac, who defeated the militant Indigenous people and the Americans to preserve New France, were all great statesmen. So was the third British governor, Sir Guy Carleton, Lord Dorchester, who was absent four years in London lobbying for passage of the Quebec Act, finally adopted in 1774, just before the outbreak of the American revolution. The Quebec Act guaranteed the linguistic, religious, and civil legal rights of the French Canadians in exchange for adherence to the British crown. Without that allegiance, Canada would undoubtedly have been taken over by the American insurrectionists, who were represented in this country by the redoubtable Benjamin Franklin and by an army headed by the then loyal revolutionary, Benedict Arnold. As it was, Canada, strenuously defended by the French Canadians and the small British garrison, narrowly survived the Revolutionary War and the War of 1812 thirty years later.

From the end of the War of 1812 (1815) for fifty years, as the United States was walking on eggshells toward, and then marching determinedly through the Civil War, internally tangled and preoccupied with the problems between the slave and free states, Canada had a great deal to accomplish to get itself to a position of plausible candidacy for autonomous statehood. It was just a string of adjacent settlements that did not happen to be American: British and French colonies in Nova Scotia, New Brunswick, and Quebec; and an infusion of fugitives from the American Revolution in Quebec and Ontario (created as the province of Upper Canada by Carleton in 1791). There was no particular affinity between the French and English Canadians, and almost no point of contact between them, and their legislatures effectively had only the authority of municipalities. The British were in the habit of sending as governors be-medalled veterans of the Napoleonic Wars who tended to be pigheaded, authoritarian Francophobes.

Canadians had to have approximately the same civil rights and power to elect those who governed in all domestic-policy areas as their British and American analogues, or they would revolt as the Americans had, and the Americans would be delighted to receive them into their ever-expanding, though divided union. There was immense unrest in Britain for an expanded and more equitable franchise, resulting in the first Reform Act, of 1832. Canadians could not long suffer to be told that their entitlements were inferior. The matter was resolved in what would become a vintage Canadian manner. The insensitive and occasionally oppressive conduct of these often unsuitable governors produced the Gilbert and Sullivan rebellions of William Lyon Mackenzie in Upper

Canada (Ontario) and Louis-Joseph Papineau in Lower Canada (Quebec) in 1837. The rebellions were really just a gang of unruly hotheads in a tavern north of Toronto, and a few earnest petitioners in Quebec, in the exaggerated style of the French National Convention of the 1790s, and they were easily dispersed.

The Canadians had arisen just vigorously enough to get the attention of the British, who had some sense of loyalty to the principal component of the English-speaking Canadian population who had fled the American colonies rather than depart British rule. And the 1837 rebellions were not sufficiently brusque to move the British to give Canada, for which it had little practical use at this point, to the United States for some less troublesome consideration, such as joint ownership of the isthmian canal that was already in contemplation for what became Panama (when U.S. president Theodore Roosevelt incited the secession of that Colombian province 65 years later). The task of the Canadians was to agitate sufficiently for Britain to grant them the civic prerogatives enjoyed by British and American citizens, but not so clangorously that Britain felt overburdened by its implicit military guaranty of Canada, which was all that deterred the Americans from taking it over. The War of 1812 was absolutely the last date when the United States would have had a substantial military problem doing so.

A reformer, Lord Durham, was dispatched in 1840 as governor, to recommend a resolution of the mysterious Canadian discontentment. He deferred the main issue of autonomous rule in domestic matters, "responsible government," but thought that the disgruntlement of the French should be addressed by relieving them of the supposedly intolerable burden of being French by assimilating them. To this end, Lower and Upper Canada were combined to form the United Province of Canada, which had a slight Anglophone majority that was unofficially charged with acculturating its French-speaking countrymen.

Durham was quickly sacked for exceeding his authority but his report was implemented. Again, a magnificent Canadian outcome: the political leaders of the two Canadas, Robert Baldwin and Louis-Hippolyte LaFontaine, made common cause in peaceful agitation for home rule, i.e., responsible government by an elected legislature, until the newly installed monarch, Queen Victoria, sent out the enlightened governor Lord Elgin, with orders to give the Canadians their rights. Baldwin and LaFontaine produced responsible government, secularized for development of immense tracts of property that had been reserved to the Church of England, and assured that the University of Toronto would be multi-sectarian.[1] This was Canada's participation in the immense international political upheaval of 1848 that brought back the Bonapartes in France, sent the long-serving Chancellor Metternich packing in Vienna, and led to widespread uprisings in Europe and as far afield as Brazil. Revolution was in the air and Canada responded, as it always does, with moderation. Having accomplished their purposes, Baldwin and

---

1 At times, the skullduggery of the British governors caused first Baldwin and then LaFontaine to be defeated in their constituencies, but each had his partner elected in his own area, so LaFontaine sat a term for northern Toronto and Baldwin represented Rimouski on the lower St. Lawrence, where he had never been and which was entirely French, a language with which Baldwin had only the remotest familiarity.

LaFontaine, as incorruptible as Cincinnatus and Washington, withdrew from public life.

They had scarcely withdrawn from it when there emerged the man who would dominate the emergence of the meta-morphosing country for thirty-five years and lead its establishment as a sovereign state, albeit sheltered by Great Britain as a "dominion," a term given political application for the first time. Champlain's seventeenth-century dream of a French Laurentia, which fit into Carleton's eighteenth-century dream of a French and British state flourishing to the north of the Americans, had survived and was almost ripe, a remarkable achievement in itself.

* * *

John A. Macdonald was co-leader of the United Province and prime minister of the Dominion of Canada for a total of twenty-eight years. He was the principal inspiration for the notion of Confederation and although he knew little about Quebec, he realized that the key to making a country out of all this debris of colonialism was a double veto on great projects and issues. On very important matters, there must be a majority among both language groups. He saw, as his more perceptive successors in the headship of the Canadian government did also, that if it became a matter of the English simply imposing their numerical superiority on the French, the Confederation he was fashioning through the 1860s would crack up.

Macdonald sold his ideas to enough Canadians, ham-mered them out at conferences in Charlottetown and Quebec, sold them to both parties in London, and to Disraeli and Gladstone personally, and maintained cordial relations with President Lincoln. The end of the U.S. Civil War and the assassination of Lincoln gave the Canadian progress to confederation a special urgency. The United States now possessed, in the Grand Army of the Republic, the greatest army in the world, and the greatest generals also, and post-Lincoln America was unencumbered with any reservoir of goodwill for Britain, most of whose leaders had overtly favoured the Southern Confederacy in the late war. Macdonald's French-Canadian associate in the project was George-Étienne Cartier (named George because of his parents' admiration of King George III, against whom the Americans had rebelled), and together they put confederation through with Victoria's blessing, under Disraeli's leadership of the House of Commons, in a break in the tumultuous debate of the Second Reform Act, which greatly expanded the British electorate again in 1867.

Macdonald would bind the country together with a miraculous railway, built with great difficulty over the Canadian Shield much of the way, and largely financed by the federal government, reviving Jean Talon's strategy of private- and public-sector collaboration in nation-building. He established Canada as a serious and autonomous neighbour of the United States by his robust stance at the Washington conference of 1871, where the British had to be steadily stiffened and propped up to avoid a complete capitulation as they resumed peaceful relations with the Americans. The United States did not really take Canadian sovereignty seriously and the British, after the founding of the united German Empire by Bismarck earlier in 1871, were determined to appease and conciliate every other Great Power, given the sudden emergence of Germany as the greatest state in Europe after its defeat of France in the Franco-Prussian War.

Macdonald had to deal with many secessionist threats, including the Metis in 1885, which he used to gain approval of the last slice of financing for the railway, having credited that project with saving the country by the rapid dispatch of troops to quell the uprising. This was the splendid achievement of using two crises to solve each other. Macdonald died in office in 1891, the head of a stable and rising country. Even in the times of Lincoln, Palmerston, Bismarck, Disraeli, and Gladstone, he was a great statesman and was seen as such by all of them except Bismarck (they had no exposure to each other).

Yet, at time of writing, Macdonald has just been demoted from Canada's ten-dollar bill, from single occupancy of one side to sharing his position with Cartier and gender and native tokens who are worthy people but not of the stature to put on a banknote. Macdonald's name has been voted to be removed from the law faculty building of Queen's University in his native Kingston, and he is regularly burned in effigy by militant Indigenous groups, though he was not hostile to Indigenous people. Rather, he gave them the right to vote and had many Indigenous allies, including the Cree and Blackfoot chiefs Poundmaker and Crowfoot. This sort of reflexive self-consciousness remains an aspect of the Canadian political culture, partly from an ignorance of the country's history. Americans and some other eminent nationalities may be insufficiently historically self-critical; Canada has the reverse problem. The country was a well-launched dominion, midway between a colony and a completely independent country, when Macdonald died in 1891.

* * *

In the next election after Macdonald's death, his party was replaced by the Liberals, led by Wilfrid Laurier, who would serve fifteen consecutive years as prime minister and prove to be a statesman of approximately equivalent stature to Macdonald. Laurier was elected despite the Conservatives promising more generous schooling than did Laurier for Roman Catholic (mainly French-speaking) families in the territories of Alberta and Saskatchewan, about to be admitted as provinces. The Conservative leader, the estimable Sir Charles Tupper, who had been a founder of Confederation from Nova Scotia and Macdonald's minister of railways and canals and high commissioner in London, hoped Quebec, which had voted narrowly for Macdonald over Laurier in 1891, would vote as Roman Catholics rather than as French Canadians. They did not, but Laurier managed an elegant compromise on the western schools, ultimately accepted by Pope Leo XIII. Laurier declined to send regular forces to support Britain in the South African War, where the enemy Boers, despite their racism and philistinism, had attracted considerable unofficial support, including from Britain's rival Germany and the colonial skeptics of America, which had just scooped up Puerto Rico, Cuba, and the Philippines in what Theodore Roosevelt had called the "splendid little war" with Spain. Roosevelt, oblivious to the well-publicized fact that Canada had become an independent country twenty years before, also described Canadians as colonists who "remain in a position which is distinctly inferior to (their) cousins in England and in the United States. The Englishman at bottom looks down on the Canadian, as he does on anyone who admits his inferiority, and quite properly too. The American, on the other hand, with equal propriety, regards the Canadian with the good-natured condescension always felt by the freeman for the land that is not free."

Obviously, Canada has made its point these 130 years, but Canadians generally suspect that the British regard us as innocuously indistinct, a worthy but unexciting cousin, just as they suspect that Americans think of us as an inoffensive Christmas card, and of themselves as a great honking train roaring through world history. These were and are caricatures, but there is some truth to them, as with all good caricatures. Ultimately, Canada's battle is not for the hearts and minds of the British or the Americans or anyone—except themselves, and this is where the problem lies.

Canada was still dissatisfied with its status at the start of the twentieth century, and to a lesser but perceptible degree it remains so, essentially for the same reason of indistinctness in the perceptions of others and of Canadians themselves. In the fifty years from the end of the U.S. Civil War to World War I, the United States almost tripled in population, and although it was already one of the largest national economies in the world at the start of that period, it put up astonishing growth rates throughout this time and became overwhelmingly the financial, commercial, and raw materials superpower of the world.

Where Macdonald had had to set up and launch the new country, Laurier's implacable task was to keep pace with that great American surge, and he did so. He and his minister for immigration, Clifford Sifton, advertised throughout the British Isles and Central and Eastern Europe for immigration, promising free passage to the west of Canada and grants of

180 acres of land for the purposes of productive agriculture. They took the land from the original grant to the Canadian Pacific Railway and used the steamship lines that Canadian Pacific had established from Quebec and Vancouver to Europe and Japan to bring the converts to Canada. Posters of vast wheat fields with towering mountains in the distance, and of the Great Lakes and the St. Lawrence and other manifestations of the physical grandeur of Canada attracted British and Germans and were very compelling to the oppressed peasants of Russia, Ukraine, Belarus, and to the south Slavs, as well as to the lower-income people of Greece and Italy.

Here again, as with Jean Talon, and Macdonald with Canadian Pacific, private and public sectors usefully cooperated. Annual Canadian immigration figures moved steadily upwards to a peak in 1913, two years after Laurier left office, of 402,000, in a population of a little over seven million. Canada's population at the end of the U.S. Civil War was about one-fourteenth that of its neighbour, but it firmed up to one-twelfth by the start of World War I. American growth startled and inspired the world. That Canada managed to keep pace with it, demographically and economically, was scarcely noticed, but given its unglamorous, unheralded nature, that was a greater achievement, if a proportionately smaller one. The mighty United States welcomed the wretched of the world under the lamp of Lady Liberty in the greatest harbour in the world at the astounding and wonderful metropolis of New York. Canada received paid fugitives from the sclerosis and incivility of the old world, up the mighty but somewhat savage St. Lawrence to ports and destinations that in the consciousness of Europe were as remote as the far side of the moon.

Laurier greatly raised Canada's position in the British Empire and the world by becoming the leader of the opposition to British colonial secretary Joseph Chamberlain's plan for financial and military integration of the empire. On behalf of Canada, Australia, South Africa, and New Zealand, Laurier gently demurred that Chamberlain's scheme amounted to a British bid to rifle the dominions under the stress of its competition with Germany. Chamberlain privately dismissed the elegant and mellifluous Laurier as the "dancing master," but the London press recognized him as the leading figure at the conference observing the Diamond Jubilee (sixty years) of Her Imperial Britannic Majesty, Victoria, Queen and Empress. Laurier also broke new ground in meeting, as a sovereign head of government, with the president of France, and also with the pope. Every cubit of stature helped. Much remained to be had.

Laurier's greatest service to Canada was in the stance he took in World War I as leader of the opposition. He had been defeated in 1911 by Robert Borden's Conservatives, who were assisted in Quebec by that province's Nationalists, led by Papineau's grandson Henri Bourassa, who opposed Laurier's advocacy of substantial free trade with the United States. As World War I dragged on, Borden gave way to pressures for conscription and recruited many English-speaking Liberals to join him in a wartime coalition government. Laurier declined, though he continued to give strong support to the war effort. He warned Borden that if he used the English-speaking majority in parliament to impose conscription on French Canada, which saw little distinction between the combatants and had no filial loyalty to the French or English, he, Laurier, would not be able to retain the fealty of Quebec to Confederation and his following would desert to Bourassa and threaten secession. He knew that Borden would win if he called an election on the issue, but Laurier believed he could at least maintain Quebec's adherence to Canada.

A capable and decent Nova Scotian who did not have the remotest notion of the contending forces in Quebec, Borden held the election in 1917 and won with his coalition, but Laurier carried every French-speaking constituency in Canada, including ten in Ontario, New Brunswick, and Manitoba. Laurier's predictions were correct, including, privately, that the Conservatives would not win in Quebec again for an entire generation, virtually installing his Liberal Party in power. Borden acquitted himself well at the Paris Peace Conference, retired, and the Liberals, under their next four leaders, William Lyon Mackenzie King, Louis S. St. Laurent, Lester B. Pearson, and Pierre E. Trudeau, governed for fifty-one of the sixty-three years following the next federal election in 1921.

* * *

Any casual observer of international affairs of this era can see that the immense Hegelian struggle between the artificially polarized right and left had already started to come to a standstill, a stasis, somewhat on the conservative side of the spectrum. The enlightened conservative response to the demands of equality on the perfect autonomy of liberty led to the welfare programs of the West, beginning with Bismarck buying off the working class and giving security to the bourgeoisie at little fiscal inconvenience to the landed aristocracy or the great industrialists and financiers. Disraeli and Gladstone moved cautiously along parallel lines at about the same time, and Britain's David Lloyd George moved the ball a little further in the last years before the Great War.

The after-effects of that war and the impetuous, even churlish return of the United States to isolationist societal hedonism after Woodrow Wilson had excited the world with notions of world government and long-term peace produced such extreme strains that the governments of most leading nations were convulsed or overthrown. Russia had already been seized by the Bolshevik Communists in 1917, but Lenin had bowed to the distasteful and temporarily renounced world revolution and confined the USSR to authoritarian socialism in 1921. The onset of the Great Depression and the morbid vagaries of Stalin's personality and leadership style emboldened him to starve the independent farmers *en masse* and engage in colossal purges on the merest hearsay or suspicion, terrorizing the entire Soviet population of about 140 million people.

Germany fell under the absolute dictatorship of Hitler and the National Socialists. Independent wealth was tolerated by the Nazis, as long as industry and finance were conducted in strict obedience to state policy. Enemies of the regime were exterminated. Mussolini's dictatorship in Italy did not change much and it ensured that no one starved. France had more unstable governments than usual in the Third Republic, and Britain was reduced to a coalition sponsored by the king, which enabled a socialist minority to preside over an ineffectual government of half measures. China and Spain descended into civil wars, compounded in the case of China by the barbarous invasion of Japan, an iron-fisted military dictatorship. Apart from Hitler and Stalin, the only Great Power that was led by an astute and purposeful chief who was more than equal to the challenges of the time was Franklin D. Roosevelt's America. He introduced a safety net of unemployment insurance and national pensions, and absorbed the unemployed in vast workfare projects and the recovery that was induced by public-sector spending. Canada's R. B. Bennett, the only serious interloper in the reign of Mackenzie King from 1921 to 1948, imitated Roosevelt but his reforms were struck down as unconstitutional trespasses in provincial jurisdiction. In fact, vast expanses of defence production by almost all advanced countries in preparation for an even more violent conflict than World War I administered the coup de grace to the Depression.

The grandson of William Lyon Mackenzie, W. L. Mackenzie King governed through the twenties, with a brief interruption when he came second to Arthur Meighen, Borden's successor as Conservative leader. King had been a leading English-Canadian opponent of conscription, and he would prove an extremely improbable yet successful Liberal leader. He was an academic, spiritualist bachelor who communed with the dead and effectively worshipped his ancestors along with the Christian God.

Although he lost that election to Meighen, he clung to office until he was defeated in parliament by a confidence motion and was denied dissolution in a controversial decision by the governor general, Lord Byng. King next defeated Meighen in parliament and portrayed the ensuing election as a contest for Canadian sovereignty. Byng's ruling, he said, had been an affront to Canadian nationhood. A little national self-assertion went a long way, then even more than now, and King was re-elected, only to be defeated again in 1930, having misunderstood the proportions of the Great Depression. Out of step this one time with general opinion, he had called the unemployed "slackers," among other flourishes. He sat out the next five years contentedly and, on returning to office in 1935, coasted on the coattails of Franklin D. Roosevelt's recovery and steered Canada out of the economic abyss, with little imagination and no flamboyance.

King was an early supporter of appeasement, and had urged Canada's representative at the League of Nations to repeat what was tiresomely referred to as "the Canada speech" to the effect that Canada offended no one and was far away from any troubles. King called upon Hitler, von Ribbentrop, and Goering in Berlin in 1938, and told the German führer that having been born in Berlin, Ontario (the pre-war Kitchener), he understood German sensibilities. King gave Hitler a copy of the authorized biography of himself and found the fuehrer decent, gentle, persuasive, almost hypnotic, and rather pastoral. What the Nazi leaders must have thought of this unworldly visitor from the distant reaches of the British Empire must remain a matter of unlimited bemused imagining.

With his preternatural sense of survival, King snapped out of appeasement well before the British and French leaders and early in 1939 told Canada to be prepared to play its part in a world conflagration. When war came, and the nationalist Quebec premier Maurice Duplessis called a provincial election on the issue of participation in the war, flirting with neutralist (albeit anti-Nazi) sentiment, King encouraged his Quebec ministers to intervene and promise no conscription for overseas service but full Quebec support for the war effort if Duplessis was defeated. If Duplessis were re-elected, there could be no guaranty against conscription. Duplessis lost.

In the phoney-war days of January 1940, the fractious premier of Ontario, Mitchell Hepburn, criticized King for inadequate contribution to the war effort. Hepburn said that "King must go" and King, who had already called parliament, transformed the speech from the throne into an announcement that parliament was dissolved for new elections. "King will go—to the people," he said. He won an overwhelming victory over a flustered opposition and awaited the thunder that broke over Europe a few weeks later with his government entirely renewed and war-ready, and his most formidable domestic opponents, Duplessis and Hepburn, laid low. The British ejected Neville Chamberlain (Joseph's son) and elevated Winston Churchill. Mussolini's Italy stabbed the Allies in the back (as Roosevelt put it in a world broadcast). France collapsed and the forty-nine-year-old brigadier general Charles de Gaulle fetched up in England and "assumed France" at the head of a few hundred Frenchmen, declaring his country had "lost a battle but not the war." Roosevelt put on the most agile display of political cunning and virtuosity in American history by breaking a tradition as old as his republic in successfully seeking a third presidential term. And W. L. M. King watched it all from sleepy Ottawa in a state of natural concern for the deteriorating world but serene incumbency. He was ready for the supreme crisis of Western civilization, and would prove a brilliant war leader in his inimitable fashion.

In late 1939, King negotiated the British Commonwealth Air Training Plan that trained up 130,000 aviators and in-flight personnel for the Commonwealth air forces in sixty-four training centres across Canada. It was a very imaginative plan and was wholly successful. King also pursued a navy that would be decisive in winning the Battle of the Atlantic against German submarines that threatened, in 1941 and again in 1942, to strangle the British Isles. Canada built and deployed hundreds of anti-submarine vessels and at the end of the war had, in number of ships and personnel, the third navy in the world, though this was in large part because the Germans had destroyed the Russian navy, the French had scuttled themselves, the British had destroyed the German and Italian navies, and the United States had obliterated the Japanese navy. The circumstances were peculiar and transitory but it was remarkable that Canada, which in the First World War was operating on Borden's nonsensical idea of contributing ships to the British navy, to be built in British yards and manned by British sailors, emerged from World War II with the third navy in the world, and probably the fourth air force.

The greatest accolade that had yet been accorded Canada came when the American secretary of state Cordell Hull got King out of a cabinet meeting on May 26, 1940, and said that President Roosevelt wished to say something to him so urgent that it could not be committed to writing or uttered over the telephone and asked for the immediate dispatch of someone whom, as Hull put it, "you trust as much as you trust yourself." King sent the secretary of the war cabinet, Hugh L. Keenleyside, by airplane at once, and he returned with the information that Roosevelt considered that France was finished and that he was not convinced that Britain could sustain a swift assault from Germany. He wanted King to appeal to Churchill on the basis that he was speaking for the Commonwealth dominions who urged that Britain fight as long as it could, and if it could not sustain the fight any longer, to evacuate the Royal Family and the government and that the United States would help protect the empire and sustain the Royal Navy. King sent Keenleyside back saying that he would not purport to speak for the other dominions who would immediately see it as King just being a stooge for Roosevelt, but that he would, for his own account, go as far as he thought appropriate.

* * *

In this brief, shining moment, as the Dunkirk evacuations began rescuing 338,000 British and French soldiers from the jaws of the German army, Mackenzie King, in his twenty-second year as Liberal leader and fifteenth as prime minister, briefly knew the two greatest titans of Western democracy since Lincoln and the two men upon whom the future of democratic civilization now rested, better than they knew each other. Churchill and Roosevelt had met in 1919 but Roosevelt did not remember Churchill kindly, and Churchill did not remember Roosevelt at all. They had been corresponding since Churchill returned to the Admiralty at the outbreak of the war. Macdonald and Laurier had known the British leaders of their time and Borden had also met Taft and Wilson cordially. But King, who came to office before there was Canadian representation anywhere abroad except London, and who negotiated Canada's first treaty (about halibut fisheries in 1923), was now the conciliator between two of the titanic figures of world history. He wrote to

Churchill that Roosevelt thought France was likely to drop out of the war, and that while optimistic about Britain, he wished Churchill to know that if the home islands were ultimately overrun before the United States could enter directly into the war at the side of Britain and Canada, the United States would maintain the British fleet and merchant marine and worldwide interests and would impose a blockade on Europe and enter the war at the first legitimate opportunity.

This was taking a considerable liberty with what Roosevelt had said, as he had never been so precise about the U.S. entering the war and was about to conduct a memorable re-election campaign on the promise of peace through strength: "Your president says this nation is not going to war." But Roosevelt raised no objection when he saw the message. King had taken Roosevelt's idea, which would have seriously irritated Churchill at Britain's darkest hour, and scandalized the other dominions, and reformulated it in a way that was useful to Churchill. King's message arrived in London on June 1, 1940 and Churchill gave one of his great Demosthenean addresses to the world on June 4, including a passage, which King believed, almost certainly correctly, that he had inspired. After a memorable recitation of British topography and the air and sea as places where Britain would fight to defend its island home, he said, with almost hypnotic force: "We shall never surrender, and if, which I do not for one moment believe, this island or a large part of it were subjugated and starving, then our Empire beyond the seas, armed and guarded by the British fleet, would carry on the struggle until in God's good time, the New World, with all its power and might, steps forth to the rescue and the liberation of the old."

What was a fairly crass statement of implicit defeatism from Roosevelt was transformed by King into words of reassurance supremely worded and delivered to the whole world by Churchill. It was of the nature of King and of the times that King wrote in his diary that "I am quite sure that . . . I shall receive an appreciative word of thanks from [Churchill]." In fact, on June 5, Churchill warned King "not to let Americans view too complacently prospects of a British collapse out of which they would get the British fleet and the guardianship of the British Empire, minus Great Britain." Churchill's stance and the rescue of the British army stirred Roosevelt to ignore the constitutional niceties and the restrictive neutrality laws and impending election campaign and send Britain, by American vessels, 500,000 rifles, 900 artillery pieces, 50,000 machine guns, and 130 million rounds of ammunition. Unarmed on their return from Dunkirk, the British were now ready to fight on the beaches and throughout their kingdom.

Churchill was eventually moved by the word of his high commissioner in Ottawa, Sir Gerald Campbell, to write King a warm letter of appreciation on September 12, 1940. After their meeting at Placentia Bay, Newfoundland, in August 1941, King's importance to Churchill and Roosevelt declined. They got on very smoothly, and had many shared interests, though their strategic visions and the growing disparity in their countries' military and economic power somewhat reduced the coziness that prevailed from 1941 to 1943, when Britain was the senior warrior and American industrial and demographic might had not yet grown to unheard-of proportions.

Canada settled into the war. Apart from the sacrifice of half of a Canadian brigade by the British at Dieppe in 1942, ostensibly to learn more about how to invade Northern

Europe, but really just an insane sacrifice of several thousand first-class Canadian troops to create an appearance of action, all was quiet as Canada trained aircrews, sank German U-boats, and prepared to send six full divisions of volunteers to Europe. The contribution of the British dominions to the First and Second World Wars was unprecedented. Canada, Australia, New Zealand, South Africa, the British Indian Empire (India, Pakistan, Bangladesh, Myanmar, Sri Lanka, Nepal, and Bhutan), and the British West Indies contributed almost five million men, almost all volunteers, to the Commonwealth military contingent, enabling Britain to approach American manpower totals. All this even though none of these constituent Commonwealth countries was under the slightest threat apart from during the first six months of the Pacific War, after which the great American naval victories of Coral Sea and Midway and Roosevelt's immense naval construction program effectively prevented any possible Japanese invasion of Australia and New Zealand.

King's tour de force in World War II was to keep the government's promise to Quebec not to impose conscription for overseas service. As the war wore on, and although Canada had very few troops in armed combat on the ground until the invasion of Italy in the late summer and into the autumn of 1943, English Canada became absurdly worked up about the imposition of conscription, as in 1917. Both Churchill and Roosevelt knew Canada somewhat and they offered King their gratuitous advice on how to deal with the conscription question. Full of good intentions, Churchill advised King when he visited Ottawa at the end of 1941, to give the official opposition "a look-in" on the government, i.e., a coalition, which is what he led. Churchill had no idea that bringing

Conservatives into the government would lead to a cabinet majority to impose conscription and the country would split apart as it would have without Laurier in 1917--1918.

King anaesthetized, prolonged, evaded, and ultimately obfuscated, and wartime conscription for overseas service was never imposed. In one of his few serious miscalculations of Canadian public opinion, King made the statement, "Conscription if necessary but not necessarily conscription," and called a referendum in April 1942 to release the government from its pledge to avoid a draft. Even King's protegé, Quebec premier Adélard Godbout, and his powerful ally the primate of the Canadian Roman Catholic Church, Jean-Marie-Rodrigue Cardinal Villeneuve, archbishop of Quebec, who had banished anti-participationist clergy to monasteries and outspokenly supported the war effort and praised the British and Americans, sat this one out. In vain did King claim he was only seeking the same powers as those possessed by Roosevelt and Churchill. Most English-Canadian Liberal politicians were warming their constituents to chase down the Quebecois and ship them off to war where English-Canadian officers could shout at them in English. Canada voted about sixty-six per cent to release the government from its non-conscription pledge while Quebec voted over seventy-two per cent against. (About 80 per cent of English-speaking Canadians were in favour, and 90 per cent of French Canadians were opposed.) It was a disaster, but King ignored it. Nothing happened. He found Roosevelt's note of consolation saying not to worry because the French Canadians would soon be dispersed about the country and assimilated, as Franco-Americans had been, as esoteric as Churchill's unsolicited advice for a coalition government.

King negotiated an absolute guaranty of Canada's territorial integrity by the United States at Ogdensburg, in 1940, lightly disgruntling Churchill, who still in his heart fancied Canada to be "the premier Dominion of the crown." King also promised best Canadian efforts to ensure that no other power made its way across Canada or Canadian airspace to attack the United States. Thus effortlessly and in the middle of the Battle of Britain and Roosevelt's pursuit of re-election, King added the blank cheque of American protection to two centuries of British assurance of Canada against aggression. He had achieved the ultimate inviolability of Canada's vast and rich territory through the benignity of the 3,000-mile border and the protection of the world's two greatest navies. As one who imputed divine intervention to his dog's indispositions and his own bowel movements, King saw "the Hand of Destiny . . . as clearly as anything in this world could possibly be . . . a converging of the streams of influence over a hundred years as to place and time and of life purpose in the case of Roosevelt and myself."

It is easy to mock King's spirituality and it was certainly eccentric, yet none of it is strictly relevant to King's performance in office. Withal, he was the perfect and indispensable person for the great task he faced. He knew to reject Roosevelt's request to set up U.S. military bases in Canada, and to decline Churchill's mad request that King come and sit in London in the war cabinet as the South African Field Marshal Smuts did (and was turned out of office after the war, as was Churchill). King had presciently stated in parliament as France left the war: "The tragic fate of France delegates to French Canada the duty of carrying high the traditions of French culture and civilization and its burning love of liberty." He early saw both the political importance of Charles de Gaulle and what the general described in another context as "the dramatic character of my mission."

Apart from the fact that Canada had less than one-tenth of the population of the United States and one-quarter of that of the United Kingdom, Mackenzie King had two problems as the champion of the Canadian interest. He was concentrating all his efforts on being more intimate with Churchill and Roosevelt, which prevented King from making common cause in agitation with the Australians and Free French. And King was not an inspirational leader. He had no presentational flair and was not a galvanizing orator like Churchill, Roosevelt, or de Gaulle. One of King's strengths, perfectly mirroring the country he led, was his indistinctness, his uncanny ability, half calculation and half intuition, to place himself at the radical centre between poles. This strength was essential to governing Canada, still a fragile political concept, stretched between British traditions, French-Canadian reticence, and the positive and negative impact of what King described to de Gaulle as "the overwhelming contiguity" of the United States.

For all of its history, the world's great statesmen had at least been aware of Canada. Champlain's father was a close friend of King Henry IV, and the brilliant and all-powerful prime minister Cardinal Richelieu was a shareholder in his company for the development of New France, while Richelieu's "Grey Eminence," Joseph du Tremblay, was the editor of one of Champlain's books. Frontenac's wife was a chum and court intimate of Louis XIV's queen. Various British governors were close comrades of the Duke of Wellington, and Victoria's son, son-in-law, and grandson (the Duke of

Connaught, Marquess of Lorne, and Earl of Athlone), were all governors general. But Churchill and Roosevelt actually knew Canada. Churchill crossed it on an author's tour and again when he resigned as chancellor in 1929, and was so impressed by the Rocky Mountains that he wrote to his wife that he would be tempted to emigrate and make some money in Canada if Neville Chamberlain gained in control of the British Conservative Party. Roosevelt's family had a cottage on Campobello Island, New Brunswick, which is where he was stricken by polio (presumably contracted in New York). He had sailed all along the Canadian Atlantic coast and after an absence of twelve years he captained his own sailboat through the fog off Maine and New Brunswick as president in 1933 and called out by name many people onshore as he eased his vessel up to the dock. As governor of New York, he had been to Toronto and Montreal and studied the public power authority of Ontario. This, too, was an augmentation of Canada's status: the world's greatest leaders knew something about it.

But they knew nothing of its politics and, in fact, did not know it at all other than as a relatively serene and rich country broadly aligned with their policies in the world. No one really knew Canada, including most Canadians, in the sense of the national essence and vocation, and although Canada has steadily progressed, with a remarkable absence of national disasters or even serious setbacks, it still does not, as a nation, know its history or assess seriously its prospects. None of this prevented Mackenzie King from leading Canada to a brilliant war, and being re-elected for a fifth full term as prime minister as Roosevelt died, Churchill was defeated at the polls, and de Gaulle resigned (though the latter two would be back). King sympathized with his illustrious allies but recorded that he and Stalin were now the world's senior leaders, "and of course, I have led my party longer than he has."

* * *

Stalin, a cunning and psychotic leader, made the same mistake as German Emperor Wilhelm II when he attacked American merchant ships on the high seas, and as Japan made when it attacked Pearl Harbor: he chronically underestimated the United States. He also seems to have bought into some of the Marxist nonsense. The United States was and remains incomparably the most powerful country in the world (which makes Canada's achievement in roughly keeping pace with it in demography and prosperity the more impressive). Once American leaders realized they were in a worldwide competition with the Kremlin, they took full advantage of being leader of the Free World (even if many of its early allies, such as Franco's Spain, Syngman Rhee's South Korea, and the Shah's Iran, were autocratic governments) to hype capitalism in theory and, through massive assistance, to put Western Europe back on its feet. Democracy spread and capitalism, as the only economic system that caters to the almost universal human desire for more, easily outdistanced the sluggish and corrupt and often brutal Marxists.

The astounding Mackenzie King was so impressed by Winston Churchill's address in President Harry S. Truman's home state of Missouri, at Fulton College in April 1946, that he telephoned Churchill to congratulate him, even as Truman was worrying about Stalin finding the speech provocative (it introduced the "iron curtain" metaphor to warn of Soviet Russia's imperial ambitions). Churchill did King the honour, completely unprecedented in Canadian and perhaps British history, of asking him to call his opponent, British prime minister Clement Attlee, and assure him that Churchill had not embarrassed Britain. King did so.

A few months earlier, Mackenzie King had accidentally fired the starting pistol in the Cold War when Soviet embassy clerk Igor Gouzenko defected to Canada and revealed the extent of Soviet espionage in the West. The prime minister travelled to Washington to brief Truman personally, and to England to do the same for Attlee. When King was ill in London, King George VI, Churchill, and Attlee all visited him in his suite in the Dorchester Hotel. He would not meet these eminent people again, and he claimed that in this last meeting with Churchill, as with Roosevelt at Quebec in 1944, Churchill had kissed him, and that Roosevelt had asked King to kiss him on the cheek. Such reminiscences should be treated with great caution, but King had personally, by his reliability as an ally and through his political endurance, helped to raise the stock of Canada immensely since the Halibut Treaty days 25 years before.

John A. Macdonald, Wilfrid Laurier, and Mackenzie King were, uninterruptedly, either co-leader of the Province of Canada, or prime minister of the Dominion (ultimately the Realm) of Canada, or leader of the opposition from 1856 to 1948, overlapping only from 1887 to 1891 when Macdonald led the government and Laurier the opposition. Between them, they led the government for sixty-five of those ninety-two years and conducted Canada from a ludicrous province officially created to assimilate the French Canadians into a bicultural federation. What began as ripe fruit for a rampaging American republic that had recently bought a million square miles from Napoleon and wrested another million square miles thirty years later from the Mexicans (in one of the most unequal wars in history), became, after these ninety-two years led by these three very different men, one of the world's twelve or so most important countries. Instead of being a bargaining chip between the British and Americans, Canada had become a vital and trusted junior ally of both.

There had been eight other prime ministers in the ninety-two years dominated by these three men, but in the same period, the United Kingdom had had seventeen prime ministers leading twenty-nine separate governments, and the United States had had nineteen presidents and twenty administrations (President Cleveland's terms were not consecutive.) Macdonald was the founder; Laurier breathed life into and personified the bicultural country, ensuring that it kept pace with the vertiginous rise of mighty America; and King navigated cautiously but flawlessly through severe economic challenges, a world war, and the start of the Cold War. It cannot be said that, as in the United States, the office sought the man, but the reverse is just as remarkable when, in Canada, the right men successfully sought and held the office. Between them, these three men won seventeen of twenty-three general elections. There is nothing remotely like this in the history of any other serious democratic country.

The idea of building a successful state in the northern half of North America—which inspired Champlain and Carleton, Baldwin and LaFontaine, and Macdonald, Laurier, and King—survived and was strengthened, but was not when King retired in 1948, and is not yet, a permanent and indestructible political fact in the world. The Great Powers do not have to take it seriously into account in its own right as they do more recently revived or fabricated nations like China, Russia, India, Germany, Japan, and Italy.

St. Laurent followed King when he retired in 1948. He was bicultural and completely respected and admired in all parts of the country throughout his professional career as a prominent lawyer, and certainly after King asked him to enter public life. He only did so as a wartime sacrifice, and he was never really a partisan figure. He was an elegant, moderate, very competent and distinguished man, a sage elder in the era of President Eisenhower, the revenant Winston Churchill, and West German chancellor Konrad Adenauer: men over sixty-five who had earned golden spurs, moving slowly toward a generational change.

John Diefenbaker, a fine parliamentarian and civil libertarian, came like a prairie fire in 1957 and 1958 but had no aptitude to govern Canada. He won a huge majority in 1958 because Maurice Duplessis, the brilliant, cunning, and ruthless premier of Quebec who dominated the public life of that province for a whole generation and who turned Quebec into a modern and prosperous jurisdiction where the state had more secular authority than the Church for the first time since the departure of the French in 1763, delivered Quebec to Diefenbaker in 1958 to avenge the King government's intervention against him in 1939.

Diefenbaker's government was reduced to a minority in 1962, and pitched altogether the next year after he crashed a meeting of U.S. president John F. Kennedy and British prime minister Harold Macmillan at the home of Canadian industrialist E. P. Taylor in the Bahamas and declared that the Western Alliance (NATO, which Canada co-founded in 1949), was reducing its dependence on nuclear weapons and that Canada would not honour its commitment to have nuclear warheads on its anti-aircraft missiles that it operated in coordination with the United States in the continental defence system (NORAD). NATO adopted no such policy and the government disintegrated. Diefenbaker was replaced by Lester B. Pearson, the Liberal leader whose succession was approved in advance by both King and St. Laurent when Pearson, a career diplomat, became external affairs minister in 1948, succeeding St. Laurent himself.

* * *

Pearson had become an international figure and an extremely distinguished Canadian public figure when, in 1956, after Britain and France, insanely, had responded to the Egyptian seizure of the Suez Canal by concerting an invasion of Egypt by Israel, which they would then use as a pretext to invade Egypt and retake the canal. At the same time, the Soviet Union militarily repressed a popular revolt against the Russian occupation of Hungary. President Eisenhower, in the midst of a re-election campaign, was not informed, but his state department generated an idea for the insertion of "peacekeepers" between the combatants, to preserve some fig leaf of dignity for the Anglo-French in this diplomatic and military disaster they had conceived and fomented, among the most horrible strategic fiascos in the rich history of either country. The American ambassador to the United Nations, Henry Cabot Lodge, gave the idea to Pearson, as he said the Russians would veto anything from the U.S. in that charged ambience. Pearson took it and lobbied very effectively for its endorsement by the UN majority. Pearson was awarded the Nobel Peace Prize, and he earned it more than most modern recipients, but this accident gave rise to a widespread and altogether unwarranted figment of the Canadian imagination that the country had some distinct national vocation and status as a peacekeeper. The Pearson–St. Laurent mediation over Suez was just the third time, after King interpreted between Churchill and Roosevelt in June 1940, and King launched the Cold War with the Gouzenko Affair in 1945, when Canada directly influenced the most important events in the world.

Pearson was an elderly diplomat on becoming prime minister, unilingual, uncharismatic, but likeable. He gave the country a distinct flag, which was contested but is now universally accepted, and a national pension scheme. He was not strong; the job often seemed too much for him and he would leave it happily after five years. But he recognized his limitations and saw clearly that there was a simmering pressure cooker in Quebec. The first Liberal leader since Edward Blake in 1887 who neither knew Quebec nor spoke French, nor had a Quebec federal associate prime minister who did, Pearson saw that Quebec could be stampeded out of the country before Canada knew there was a crisis. Quebec federalists were being heavily outgunned by fashionable nationalists, most of them separatists, in the academic and media communities of Quebec. Pearson set up a powerful commission on bilingualism and biculturalism, which soon stated that Canada was facing the greatest challenge in its history. So it was, and it was about to become worse.

Pearson called an unnecessary election in the autumn of 1965, ostensibly to win a majority, but particularly to bring to Ottawa some powerful federalist voices from Quebec. This new wave of French Quebec federalists was led by writer and academic Pierre Elliott Trudeau, labour leader Jean Marchand, and *La Presse* editor Gerard Pelletier. Pearson promoted all of them as quickly as he could. When Daniel Johnson won the 1966 Quebec election, the heat of federal-provincial discussions rose markedly. Johnson was almost as accomplished a diplomat as Pearson, and a much better politician. He was not a separatist but he had elaborated Duplessis's pursuit of "autonomy" to a precise schedule of jurisdictional concessions necessary to save federalism: "Equality or independence. That's what Quebec wants. What does Canada want? Que veut le Canada?" This was his dramatic conclusion at a provincial conference on the future of Canada convened by widely respected Ontario premier John Robarts in the autumn of 1967, Canada's centennial year.

In July of that year, Johnson had radically escalated discussions by inviting Charles de Gaulle to visit Quebec. De Gaulle was now rivaled only by Mao Tse-tung as the world's most renowned statesman, in his second term as president of the French Fifth Republic. De Gaulle came by ship so he did not have to start his visit at Ottawa, which had invited the leaders of all countries that participated in the Montreal World's Fair of 1967. De Gaulle had told Canadians when he visited Ottawa in 1960 that Canada was an accomplished country of "hard-working and enterprising people," and "solid, stable . . . orderly . . . and sensitive to human liberty and the dignity of man." In his wartime memoirs, in 1945, Canada was "heroic." But by 1967, he had set his sights on sponsoring an independent Quebec under America's nose, to be a cadet of renascent France in the New World; to sunder the world's third Anglo-Saxon power and to flex the political muscle of la Francophonie.

Johnson, who used the province's school buses to bring in crowds to line almost the entire route between Quebec and Montreal on a beautiful July 24, got more than he bargained for. There were dense crowds in East Montreal as the leaders drove to the city hall on Place Jacques-Cartier, which was jammed with scores of thousands of people waving separatist placards. De Gaulle, wearing his general's uniform, spoke from the balcony of city hall and said that the reception he had had all along his route that day reminded him of the liberation of France. He concluded, his whole great frame shaking with emotion, with an electrifying shout of the separatist slogan, *"Vive le Québec libre!"* In probably the most important oration in Canadian history up to that time, by the most eminent visitor Canada had had since Roosevelt and Churchill attended the Quebec Conferences, de Gaulle had effectively invited Quebec to secede.

Immense excitement ensued. Pearson deliberated with his cabinet for almost twenty-four hours before issuing a clear though polite rebuke, welcoming de Gaulle, applauding his generous reception, recalling Canadian sacrifices for France in both world wars, and referring to his remarks as "unacceptable." De Gaulle had never had any wish to go to Ottawa and he cancelled the rest of his visit and flew home the next day.

Pearson retired as soon as he decently could, aware that Quebec was almost out of control, and Pierre Trudeau, with Pearson's blessing and support, succeeded him. At the eleventh hour, federalism had found and elevated a mighty protagonist. Where Macdonald, Laurier, and King had sought the office, once again, as with St. Laurent, the office sought the appropriate man. The thread of Canada's raison d'être came into very purposeful hands.

* * *

Trudeau was Canada's first glamorous prime minister: stylish, intellectual, an accomplished writer and sportsman, with inherited wealth and worldliness, and unquestionable qualities of leadership. He was an authoritarian *chef* in the French-Canadian tradition, like Laurier and Duplessis. Trudeau dissolved parliament and gained the first federal majority since Diefenbaker's in 1958 by promising a "just society." He set to work building the federalist fortress.

The world was so astounded that Canada had a flamboyant leader after the relentless and somewhat geriatric sobriety of King, St. Laurent, Diefenbaker, and Pearson that Trudeau became a great international celebrity and pulled large crowds almost everywhere he went. His constitutional policy was an absolute stonewall. He would make no more concessions of jurisdiction as Pearson had done. Rather, he would promote biculturalism throughout the country. There would be access to federal government services and broadcast outlets everywhere in Canada in both official languages, and he massively augmented transfer payments and programs of economic incentives for disadvantaged regions. Apart from a few tokens in the Atlantic provinces and the prairies, this meant a Niagara of financial resources and grants inundating Quebec.

One of the tenets of the Quebec separatists was that Canada was not a real country but an Anglo-American patchwork of pretended nationality designed to mystify and divert Quebec from a sovereign French destiny reasserted after two centuries during which, as long-serving Montreal mayor Jean Drapeau said, "we had to hang our culture on the barn door." Trudeau assaulted these overstuffed and self-indulgent platitudes by publicly taking issue with the Americans, striking up a warm relationship with Fidel Castro and the Chinese leaders, and some satellite leaders in the Soviet bloc. He withdrew Canadian forces from Europe under the NATO association, advanced rather vapid proposals for arms control, and postured in the Third World, sprinkling foreign aid among former British and French colonies. He never had any concept of American political forces and to his last days had no idea why the American public preferred President Reagan to President Carter.

After de Gaulle's resignation in 1969, subsequent French leaders were much less ardent in their championship of Quebec nationalism. And in Quebec itself, the leadership was for a time less assertive. Daniel Johnson died of a coronary in 1968 at the early age of fifty-three, and his successor, Jean-Jacques Bertrand, and the next premier, Robert Bourassa, age thirty-six, were much less forceful champions of Quebec's jurisdiction than Duplessis, Jean Lesage, and Johnson had been. But Lesage's most prominent minister, René Lévesque, a former television journalist with a wide following in Quebec, bolted the Liberals after their defeat in 1966. He founded the Parti Québécois and championed sovereignty association, which promised Quebec the joys of independence and the financial comforts of confederation— essentially eating and retaining the same cake.

Around the same time, one of Canadian history's greatest church leaders, Paul-Émile Cardinal Léger, archbishop of Montreal, retired to move to Africa and build a hospital to assist lepers and other victims of tropical illnesses in underdeveloped countries. He was extremely respected in Quebec and, though a federalist, was above the disparagement of the nationalists. His departure largely eliminated any concentrated political influence of the Roman Catholic Church in Quebec, where it had played a strong and generally conservative role since Champlain founded New France. What was generally called the Quiet Revolution, ushered in by Lesage, Levesque, and others in 1960, secularized schools and hospitals. Quebec had admittedly been somewhat priest-ridden, but the Quiet Revolution had essentially the same people doing the same work in the same schools and hospitals at ten times the cost to taxpayers and with a very difficult labour-relations climate. This was one of the reasons for the defeat of Lesage by Johnson in 1966. With the death of Johnson, the nationalist torch in Quebec, which had been carried by conservatives, especially Henri Bourassa and Duplessis, passed to Levesque and the initially moderate left.

In the autumn of 1970, a terrorist separatist organization called le Front de Libération du Québec (FLQ) kidnapped first a British trade official, James Cross, and then the minister of labour of Quebec, Pierre Laporte, and murdered Laporte. Trudeau did not flinch. He imposed the outstanding statute to deal with apprehended insurrections, the War Measures Act, and effectively declared martial law in parts of Quebec. Nearly five hundred suspected subversives were rounded up in the dead of night and detained for up to ninety days and interrogated (quite civilly in all cases). It was a bit of an amateur performance, given Canada's historic lack of a need for secret police, and among those marked down to be taken into custody was Gérard Pelletier, the secretary of state who voted with the rest of the cabinet to take War Measures, as his son tried to explain to police ransacking the federal minister's house. The murderers and another cell of the FLQ were apprehended and released to go to Cuba. Cross was freed. The terrorists eventually returned and were imprisoned for a time. Trudeau handled it well and his popularity spiked for a time. However, Canada being Canada, Trudeau quickly offended a great many people by his haughty manner and seeming invulnerability and while he retained the overwhelming support of Quebec, his popularity sagged elsewhere and he almost lost power in the 1972 election. He regained his majority in 1974.

In 1976, Lévesque's Parti Québécois won the Quebec election and announced that there would be a referendum on sovereignty association in his term. Trudeau was the man to deal with this situation but, perversely, Canadians removed him in 1979, electing instead a most unlikely, though unexceptionable man, Joe Clark, as prime minister. He mishandled a confidence vote and Trudeau was back to face Lévesque in the 1980 referendum after all. Trudeau called sovereignty association a non-starter, ran a flawless campaign, and was enjoying a steady lead when finally Lévesque blew up and said Trudeau could not be trusted because his middle name was Elliott. This was all Trudeau needed, in addition to his relentless mockery of the snake oil of having independence and "association" with Canada at the same time. What Trudeau (and Duplessis and Lesage and

Johnson) realized, and Lévesque (and Charles de Gaulle) did not, was that Quebecers retain the parsimony and bourgeois conservatism of their Norman and Breton ancestors. They will ominously exude discontent and threaten dire scenarios, but if treated with respect and offered a good economic argument, as well as provincial autonomy in their agreed jurisdiction, they will not do anything impetuous. All the province was asked to do in the referendum was allow Lévesque to attempt to negotiate sovereignty and association, yet the federalists won 60 to 40 (the vote was neck and neck among French-speaking Quebecers).

It was then Trudeau's turn to deliver on his promise to patriate Canada's constitution (the British North America Act still had to be amended in Westminster, although it was a rubber-stamp procedure). One of Trudeau's astute tactics was to ridicule arguments about federal and provincial jurisdiction, as he had with Pearson and Johnson at the 1967 federal-provincial conference, while championing a charter of rights and freedoms. It enabled him to dismiss the entire federal-provincial debate as the childish bickering of greedy politicians when what was required was the entrenchment of the rights of all. It was nonsense, but an inspired invocation of an idealistic notion of the primordial and insuperable rights of everyman. Trudeau eventually made an agreement with all of the provinces except Quebec. A constitutional-amending formula confined to Canada was accepted, a Charter of Rights and Freedoms was agreed, and the British North America Act of 1867 was replaced but largely replicated by the Constitution Act of 1981. Lévesque affected great umbrage but he had not been bargaining in good faith and his humiliation was not undeserved. Trudeau had to abandon the protection of property rights in the Charter to gain the support of the NDP, the leftist party that for its first thirty years was the depression-born Cooperative Commonwealth Federation (CCF). It changed its name to the New Democratic Party in 1961 and has retained the name long after it ceased to be new.

The subscribing governments all retained the power to revoke certain court decisions that trespassed in their jurisdictions, most importantly the right of provinces to vacate federal court decisions in matters of property and civil rights. This was especially important as Quebec was already, under Bourassa, and even more under Lévesque, legislating to restrict the rights of non–French speakers. This revocation of the rights within Quebec of the English-speaking Canadian majority—rights that had been exercised in Quebec since the end of the Seven Years War—was a fundamental assault on freedom of expression. Many English-speaking Canadians were distinctly unenthused about subsidizing Quebec to the extent of more than $2,000 per capita while the province tried to suppress the usage and teaching of their language. There was a general agreement not to break out and reveal the financial cost of Quebec to Canada: the Quebec nationalists did not want to admit the proportions of the subsidy and the federalists did not want to inflame anti-Quebec opinion in the country. It was all very Canadian, and the country started to come out of the crisis.

* * *

Trudeau retired and the first bilingual Quebecer ever to lead the federal Conservatives, Brian Mulroney, won the 1984 election and for eight years pursued an ambitious program. He achieved a free trade agreement with the United States, which increased trade with that country as a percentage of GDP and shut down a lot of branch plants and enabled Canada unfettered access to the immense American market. It was generally successful and boosted Canada's self-confidence. He also adopted a federal Goods and Services Tax that began a movement of tax collection from incomes to consumption, a better and fairer and more stimulative and almost voluntary form of taxation.

Mulroney was less successful with his effort to patch Quebec entirely into confederation in what was called the Meech Lake Accord. Restrictive language measures by Robert Bourassa's government raised a tremendous backlash and the accord, failing ratification in Manitoba and Newfoundland, evaporated. Mulroney tried again with the Charlottetown Agreement, which substantially decentralized government. It was supported by every government and official opposition in the country except the Parti Québécois but it was defeated in a national referendum.

This roused in Quebec a more overtly separatist movement that rode the wave of resentment at the isolation of the province and the balking of Canada at Meech Lake and Charlottetown. A 1995 independence referendum campaign was led by Mulroney's former ambassador to Paris and environment minister, firebrand Lucien Bouchard, who took advantage of the complacency, and then the unnerved jitters of Mulroney's successor, Liberal wheel-horse Jean Chrétien. The referendum question, somewhat more explicit than in 1980, failed by only a single per cent to gain majority approval to negotiate Quebec's independence.

Quebec had made its point and shot its bolt. Over half a million Quebecois, largely English speakers, departed Quebec in thirty years, and in the great secularization of the Quiet Revolution, the birth rate collapsed. In order to maintain Quebec's population, ostensible francophones were admitted from Haiti, Maghreb (North Africa), and Lebanon. Apart from the fact that their linguistic talents, at least in comprehensible French, tended to be somewhat limited, they did not care about Quebec's ancient dreams of independence and were immigrating to a stable country and a predominantly English-speaking continent.

Without ever being explicit about what they were doing, Trudeau and Mulroney spent tens of billions of dollars over twenty-five years dispensing money raised in Ontario, Alberta, and British Columbia in Quebec, enabling that province to move to an almost entirely white-collar economy, and to be autonomous in almost every field except currency and the money supply, defence, and sovereign international relations. Quebec was seduced as its restrictive language laws drove out hundreds of thousands of non-French, opening up for the French-speaking majority higher employment echelons and more commodious residences in formerly English and Jewish districts.

The Supreme Court of Canada ruled that an act of secession would have to be on an unambiguous question and by a solid majority. Jean Chrétien passed the Clarity Act, a legislative enactment of the Supreme Court findings, to atone for his nearly catastrophic bungling of the 1995 referendum. Chrétien and his capable finance minister, Paul Martin, demonstrated that the crisis was subsiding by vacating a good many shared spending areas without ceding any additional rights to the provinces to raise revenues. The provinces responded by laying a lot off on the larger municipalities and local taxes jumped appreciably, but the extent of the interprovincial transfers was sharply reduced and Canada ran fourteen consecutive federal budget surpluses under both major parties, a record of fiscal responsibility vastly exceeding that of any other large advanced economy. Canada came through the 2008–2009 world financial crisis and recession better than any of its peers, its banking system not remotely strained, and in general, the country had sensible, prudent government for all of the period between the retirement of Pierre Trudeau in 1984 and the election of his son Justin Trudeau in 2015. Once again, Canada had come through.

Pierre Trudeau was the man of the very difficult time, as Macdonald, Laurier, and King had been in their times. And as St. Laurent had answered the call to help keep Quebec steady during World War II and had never considered entering public life before he was sixty, Trudeau entered public life in 1965, having rejected it entirely for decades as a career, to defend federalism when it was under siege. Canadians, since they should know better, are the worst offenders in the underestimation of Canada's national accomplishment in remaining together, navigating the centuries between the British and Americans, not being subsumed into the United States, and sailing into calm, sun-dappled waters at last. The mystical thread remains intact.

PART 2

THE OPPORTUNITY

The foregoing makes no pretence to being anything but a sequence of highlights and patterns in Canadian history, to assist us in considering Canada's strengths and vulnerabilities, and its prospects. I concluded my history of Canada (last published in 2016) with the prediction: "The past reveals the future." It does, and the past is distinguished, but the future could be better. The country is in no danger, and is not overly discontented. As the new millennium opened, Canada was like an awakening desert traveller, rubbing his eyes in the bright yet still cool air of morning to ensure that the absence of a threat was not a mirage. In resumé, we achieved freedom and full independence with almost no violence, and have survived the pressures of demographic and cultural absorption in the American orbit. We have fought only in just wars, always with distinction and on the winning side. When the British, for whom we had given our all in two world wars, put us over the side to plunge headlong into Europe, we got on quite well, and better than they did. We have weathered recent financial crises better than any other diversified-economy country, even as the legendary banking nations, the Swiss, the Dutch, and the Scots faltered. No country is our enemy, and when the greatest statesman in the world tried to incite the breakup of this country, to which his nation owed a great deal, we sent him packing, to the envy of the Anglo-Americans. Moreover, every knowledgeable person in the world looks on Canada benignly, and with some level of respect. No part of the country is threatening to secede, (though at time of writing, Alberta is being so grossly short-changed, there is a little talk of it).

It is magnificent, except that our progress has been so subtle and incremental that very few Canadians think it has been at all difficult or unusual since the heroics of the early explorers and settlers. And neither, naturally, since we do not tell them, do foreigners. We are much larger, and more populous and naturally richer than Scandinavia, but have no Sibelius or Ibsen, or Grieg, (and now have an inferior standard of living). Canada became a member of the G7 (the democratic world's seven leading economies), but not because the earlier members were calling out for us. Rather, because the French, Germans, and British wanted to add Italy, and the U.S. and Japan did not want to be swamped by Europeans. Within Canada, and between Canada and the world, it is always a compromise. As historian W. L. Morton wrote, it is a country "strong only in moderation and governable only by compromise."

Of course, Canada is fortunate to have the immense and rich territory that it does, despite climatic rigours at places and times. We were fortunate, as has been mentioned, to have been founded by the French, and taken over by the British as the American colonies were about to secede from the British Empire, to avoid being subsumed into America.

We were fortunate that as Canada was prising the institutions of self-government from the British, the Americans were struggling with the slavery crisis, and that when that crisis was resolved, the United States was too exhausted by war to endure the unlimited naval harassment and bombardment that would have come from the British if they had seized Canada. All this was good fortune, but everything else we did ourselves.

Most of what Canada has assembled as a nation has been accomplished by Canadians. A Canadian explored the northern Rocky Mountains: Laverendrye, from Trois-Rivières, and after he had been invalided back from France after being wounded in the Battle of Malplaquet in Louis XIV's gallant defence against the Duke of Marlborough and Eugene of Savoy. A Canadian, Marquette, explored the Mississippi River and optimistically imagined that Green Bay (Wisconsin, a football and meat-packing centre) was the gateway to China. Another Canadian, d'Iberville, also from Trois-Rivières, seized Hudson Bay from the British and Havana from the Spanish. Canadians explored the sites of what are now the American cities of Chicago, Detroit, Louisville, St. Louis, New Orleans, Des Moines, Mobile, and Biloxi. The Canadian Alexander Mackenzie, reached the Pacific in 1793, ten years before the Americans Lewis and Clark, and the Canadian Pacific Railway and Montreal's Victoria Bridge were among the engineering wonders of the world when they were completed.

Politically, Baldwin and LaFontaine's achievement in winkling responsible government from the British without exhausting Britain's enthusiasm to maintain and protect Canada; and Macdonald and others' achievement in designing a unique government, extending it across the continent

and preserving it from the covetousness of the Americans in
the West and separatist sentiment in Quebec and among the
Metis and native peoples, were astonishing, but not dramatic
accomplishments. Laurier and Sifton's success in building
immigration and economic growth to match that of the
United States was not apparently heroic; they were almost
anti-heroic, which made it even nobler and more sophisticated than growth through the simple application of force,
which was never an option for Canada. Laurier's and King's
and Trudeau's preservation of the adherence of the French
Canadians was occasionally dramatic but generally a battle
of inducements, tactics, and accommodations of French
Canada's material self-interest, which always prevailed
sensibly over mere and transitory exaltation of national self-
assertion. And now, suddenly, after four hundred years of
quiet and lonely struggle, Canada is in a healthier political
condition than any other large country.

The secret to taking Canada to new heights as a platform
for national greatness is not just more of the same. That
would build on what we have, but towards a larger model of
Scandinavia and without the national cultures that produce
more world-admired cultural figures than we do down the
lineup of both English- and French-speaking countries as we
are. We show every sign of contesting for the lead of social
democratic countries. We have officially bought entirely into
the green theory of a changing climate to be combatted by
effectively abandoning carbon emissions, although Canada's
contribution to the world's carbon emissions is a fraction of
one per cent of the total and there is no conclusive evidence
that the world is getting warmer, that climate is changing in
a way that is unusual, or that human activity has anything

to do with whatever is happening. The United States, though it has made heavy efforts in environmental activities, has withdrawn from a previous tentative commitment by the Obama administration to an immense reduction in carbon emissions, at great cost in unemployment and capping the automobile and related industries. China and India, the two greatest polluters, but both in hot pursuit of economic growth, have not committed to do anything to reduce carbon use, and neither has Russia. It is not a well-considered policy and under the Justin Trudeau government seems more of a gesture of solidarity with the social democratic group-think than a serious response to a real problem. Canada now has a minister of (environment and) climate, a Swiftian mockery of official self-importance. Until the facts of climate change and the relevance, if there is any, to human behaviour are properly established, most official activity is a pose: at best raising revenue in the name of planetary good governance; at worst, the ancient foes of capitalism coming back against it with the false claim of protecting life on earth from the primordial evil of capital accumulation, even if equitably distributed.

Another part of the effort to get to the cutting edge of social democracy has been the adjustment of spending and taxation to broaden social benefit. The goal appears to be to capitalize on the government's revenue from taxing cannabis sales and online gambling to pay for a guaranteed minimum income, and effectively demote specific social services in favour of outright grants to unemployed or underemployed adults. In the United States under the Obama administration, variations of this policy, coupled with low-cost drugs, especially tranquillizing drugs, led to a reduction of the workforce and of economic growth and an increase in the percentage of the population substantially dependent on state benefits, while deficits maintained alarming levels that were ultimately unsustainable. This is an authentic ambition and policy road map for a democratic political society. But it has been rejected in the United States and in most of Scandinavia, where it originated.

It is difficult to believe that any such program is not heavily motivated by a desire to buy votes by assuring that an immense percentage of the population is composed of welfare-dependent or substantially benefit-addicted people. Modern Western welfare systems were developed as assistance to the disadvantaged to help them become competitive, and unemployment insurance was insurance, not a substitute for employment. What we have in Canada, with contemplations of universal disbursements of income and unrepentantly high income-tax levels is perilously close to a cynical institutionalization of taking money from those who have earned it and redirecting it to those who have not, almost irrespective of merit, and in implicit exchange for their votes: one-party rule, or indistinguishable parties, with much of the population paid not to work, and the law produced by individual judges in their sinecures making up the law as they please. This is a recipe for inertia and philistinism, stagnation, and ultimately suicide.

The "green" flourish covers off part of the left, assures a high level of academic and journalistic sympathy, and harnesses what was effectively a movement toward a radical environmental policy by the international left after the collapse of the Soviet Union, the evolution of the People's Republic of China into a country of state and individual capitalism, and the heavy defeat of the domestic western left by Ronald Reagan, Margaret Thatcher, and, up to a point, Helmut Kohl and Brian Mulroney. It was a fine and spontaneous act of improvisation, as the routed left crowded onto the environmental bandwagon supported by authentic conservationists and advocates of better treatment of sewage and industrial waste and other pollutants. Suddenly, their numbers multiplied swiftly as the old left came aboard, seized the direction of environmentalism and recalibrated it as a formidable opponent to economic growth and any economic measure of progress at all. The oil and automobile and natural gas industries would have to be curtailed to reduce emissions, backing right through the industries that provide the components of an automobile, and offshore drilling, pipelines, anything that would meet the need for and cut the price of energy was environmentally unsound and had to be avoided, as the survival of the world and this country's credentials as a responsible and progressive jurisdiction had to be proven. It was a little like the leftist guerrillas who took to the jungles of Colombia decades ago after having been driven out of the metropolitan areas; in the eighties, they were suddenly joined in their tropical fastness by much more numerous and heavily armed gangs cultivating, processing, and exporting narcotics. The jungle wars retained a face of ideology and even idealism, but they were in fact a civil war with very powerful and rich crime operations. Environmentalists, wittingly or otherwise, have followed Lenin's maxim, "When you can't get in the door, use the window."

The other preoccupation of the Justin Trudeau government is in the implacable imposition of political correctness in every conceivable form, but especially in matters of gender and Indigenous people. With the connivance of its judicial appointees, and many of those inherited from the judicial choices of the preceding government of Stephen Harper, which was quite socially conservative, and the Mulroney and Chrétien and Martin governments, which were centrist, the history and official precedence of Canada was overturned in an absurdly ahistorical amplification of the status and pre-rogatives of Indigenous people. The long-serving chief justice of Canada, Beverley McLachlin, took it upon herself to apologize and express shame and guilt on behalf of Canada to the Aga Khan for attempted "cultural genocide" against Indigenous people, and for the alleged fact that "slavery was not unknown" in Canada. This was the official self-flagellating fiction that the Justin Trudeau regime invoked to turn the fiscal pockets of the country inside out and oblige federal officials to commence any public statement with a grateful acknowledgement that they are meeting and speak-ing on territory once occupied by some Indigenous tribe or band whose name was reconditely extracted from the mists of antiquity.

It was to this inane spectacle of humbling acts that the federal state of one of the world's most successful and civically virtuous countries was self-demoted just as all its traditional disquietudes and threatening fears had fallen away. There was no attempt at "cultural genocide," a prepos-terous concept—peoples can be attacked in genocides and their cultures may be discouraged, acculturated, assimilated, or even suppressed, but that would be "cultacide" or some such pestilence; no one was even attempting that in Canada. The federal government for some decades in the nineteenth and twentieth centuries was encouraging and subsidizing residential schooling delivered mainly within the private sector, especially the Christian churches. This was designed to enable Indigenous people to compete advantageously in the community of Canada as a whole, not to exterminate their consciousness of their socio-cultural roots. The policy had mixed results and there were certainly a good many instances of cruelty and incompetence, but many people thrived, and these students constituted the great majority of educated natives. It was a misconceived policy to the limited but considerable extent that it was implemented by officials who were racists and even sadists. But for the chief justice, and then the Justin Trudeau government, to tag any previous Canadian government as genocidal in any sense was an outrage and a blood libel on the English- and French-Canadian peoples.

Nor was there any slavery in Canada once Canadians had any authority to govern themselves. There were fewer than sixty slaves in New France when it was handed over to the British. They were emancipated and there were literally only a handful of slaves in all of Canada when slavery was abolished throughout the British Empire in 1832. Canada became self-governing in domestic affairs in 1848, when slavery had already been abolished. The only sizable occurrence of slavery on the territory of what is now Canada, and it was quite extensive, was among the Indigenous tribes, most of which were nomadic and had no agriculture, no permanent structures, and were chiefly preoccupied in warring with each other in sanguinary struggles that customarily ended in the sadistic execution of women and children and the enslavement of captured men. It was to Canada's great credit that it encouraged and welcomed more than 40,000 fugitive slaves from the United States in the decades prior to the U.S. Civil War. All were treated as free and were provided access to schools and social services.

There was never any question about the intelligence of Indigenous people, and they were in many ways superior in physical strength to the Europeans who came among them. In their wooden crafts (especially the construction of miraculously light and efficient canoes), in all the skills of the outdoors, and in primitive art, the Indigenous people showed their talents and keenness of mind to be entirely equal to the Europeans, but their civilization was at least five thousand years in arrears. Despite the romanticization conducted initially by writers such as Chateaubriand (*"beaux sauvages"*) and James Fenimore Cooper (*The Last of the Mohicans*), and even Longfellow in "Evangeline," their civilization was vastly inferior to the civilization of Shakespeare, Descartes, Montaigne, Leonardo, Michelangelo, and Raphael that prorupted into North America in the fifteenth and sixteenth centuries.

It is to this almost instantly discarded civilization that Canada now officially kowtows, acquiescing in the politically correct agitation for the historical demotion of John A. Macdonald, and inciting Indigenous people to badger Euro-Canadians into paroxysms of self-reproach and self-humiliation. We are invited, in effect, to accept and proclaim and repent that we are interlopers in this country and effectively invaded and occupied it, and scattered, slaughtered, and subjugated the natives, implicitly almost as Nazi Germany and Soviet Russia did the Poles in 1939. And many Indigenous people, who needed little encouragement to do so, have taken up this irresistible cause and are pushing hard on a door that has been hurled open to the point that it is straining its hinges. The territory of Canada was not remotely occupied by Indigenous people but was rather crossed over routinely in a migratory pattern by about 200,000 souls who then lived in what is even now a seriously underpopulated country of thirty-six million.

It is all a fantasy of self-hate employed by the Justin Trudeau government for reasons that can only be speculated about. No government of sane men (and women, who have to be equal in ministerial numbers, although there are many more men in the caucus—another expensive gesture) would have embarked on this extravagant farce of self-degradation while writing a blank cheque to the frequently corrupt and incompetent leaders of a large number of Indigenous sub-groups with which the government of Canada purports to negotiate, "sovereign nation to sovereign nation." Nothing useful can be accomplished by the continuation of this charade. We, the European Canadians, have substantially failed Indigenous people and we have tried earnestly, but not altogether successfully, to atone for that, fiscally and otherwise. This is a terribly complex problem, but we have to assist those who want to assimilate to the life of the country to do so while being well educated in their own history and traditions. And those who really want to remain in some replication of their original conditions must be grouped together in settlements that are large and well serviced enough to be fulfilling places to reside without the certainty of socio-phobic levels of alcoholism and violence that largely obtain now. The scandal of unaccountable misgovernment in the spurious name of Indigenous self-government must be ended.

Apart from the historic falsity of the premise for this policy, it encourages a substantially fault-free but maladjusted community to displace a will to better their lot with a sense of victimhood and entitlement and persistence in a system of unaccountable and inept self-government. In addition to disserving those it is supposed to assist, it is precisely the wrong message to give the Canadian people, who are aware of but insufficiently confident in their civic virtue and exceptionalism at steady, tolerant, mature national development despite the intimidating advantage of being historically closely linked to and physically overshadowed by the Western world's three most successful nationalities.

* * *

The national objective that would most excite the deeply recessed passions of Canadians is for their country to be generally recognized as a world leader in government, political enlightenment, equitable quality of life, and cultural attainments. To have any chance of accomplishing this, rather than drowning in the quagmire of political correctness, policies must be devised and applied in this potentially finest and most generously productive of national social laboratories. Canadians have already achieved a status as perhaps the most unquestioningly and warmly welcoming of any country to bona fide immigration. The Canadian people want Canada to be recognized and in fact envied, especially the non-French, as the temptation to set up their own country naturally lingers in the minds of the Quebecois, even when wistfully contemplating the irresistible tangible rewards of federal association.

It is impossible to imagine that any such ambitious goal as a renovated society can be accomplished by the traditional pursuit of economic, military, or demographic hegemony. There is obviously no chance of any of that, given the intimate proximity of the most successful and self-promoting nationality in the history of the world, although excellence is a legitimate and generally attainable aspiration. It may be that one of the reasons for Canada's tolerant attitude toward immigrants who legitimately wish to make their lives here and contribute to their new country, is the general awareness that we need immigration to maintain our independence from the United States, as surely as Laurier and Sifton saw it over a century ago, well into what Laurier told us, a bit prematurely, would be "Canada's century." They closed the demographic gap between Canada and the U.S. and it has now narrowed to one to nine. Canada has ninety per cent of the population France had in the *fin de siècle* when it dazzled and seduced the world with its culture of great novelists, poets, composers, sculptors, and impressionist artists, and then inspired free men everywhere with their victorious sacrifice in World War I when they twice repulsed the Germans from the gates of Paris and sustained 2,500,000 dead young men and an additional four million casualties. No one could seriously expect Canada to produce such cultural genius quickly, and even atheists will pray that no such human sacrifice is visited upon us, or on any nation, again.

The way forward to an exalted and exceptional Canadian destiny is in the elaboration of policies and structures of government and society that attract the admiration of others and are emulated. Apart from the American iconization of democracy and capitalism, this is not a formula that has been put notably to the test, at least in secular matters, since the prime of Athens. Athens was no larger than some other Greek cities, and the Athenians were generally not such fierce warriors as the Spartans, but the story of Athens has illuminated contemporary and subsequent history.

For notorious historic reasons, post-war Western Europe paid a lot of Danegeld to the working and agrarian classes to keep them orderly and not overly discontented. In this zone between almost pure capitalism and what became known as social democracy, the West, and now virtually all the developed world, has gathered, like a disparate group of wanderers making their way to a central square. It hardly needs to be emphasized that the Soviet Union peacefully disintegrated and China, while retaining its one-party autocracy, has become a largely capitalist country and has emerged as the world's second economy. India and Indonesia, the second and fourth most populous countries, have to some extent followed China in pursuit of economic growth and those countries, in particular, have enabled hundreds of millions of people to escape from poverty and illiteracy. The statistics for the upward mobility of the masses of the world have been admirable and the absence of intense Great Power rivalry has maintained a relatively calm international climate, despite the extreme nuisance of terrorism dodging among failed states and duplicitous states but never able to raise its flag over a defined territory or nationality. Practically all governments are anti-terrorist and no terrorist group can do more than duck and hide and attract the anger and hatred of almost everyone. They are not remotely a threat to the Western world, as great nations in the hands of clever and evil dictators like Nazi Germany and the Soviet Union were.

But Western liberal democracy has stalled. The United States has successfully returned to a policy of economic growth by cutting all income taxes, incentivizing the patriation of trillions of dollars of foreign profits of American corporations, emancipating businesses from strangling regulation, and fiscally encouraging investment and consumption while slashing the trade deficit it tolerated for decades for strategic reasons, and reducing petroleum imports by increasing domestic production. Immigration was largely from desperately poor and uneducated people flooding into the United States and Western Europe more like the waves of barbarians relocating onto the territory of the late Roman Empire than the conscious and purposeful immigration by families to a new and admired country with a will to assimilate to it as is celebrated at such sites as the Statue of Liberty. For the first time in the history of the world, technological advance creates more unemployment than employment. And the failure of the Western nations even to maintain their populations or for the most part to assure that immigration strengthens rather than weakens the social fibre, has, in an interesting twist, made almost all the large advanced nations of the world except the United States and Australia uncompetitive with Canada as a destination for immigration. Poverty is proving almost impossible to eliminate and, except for the United States in the freshet of the Trump capitalist Indian summer, economic growth is very sluggish. All state education systems, certainly including Canada's, have deteriorated badly and are often little better than day-care centres, and most politics in the West is mindless pandering and sloganeering.

This has been thus far an outline of who we are and how we got to where we are now. These are the ideal circumstances for Canada to transform itself into a controlled and sensible public policy laboratory and to help lead the advanced world to the next stage of its development, beyond what has become in the West a sterile left-right tug-of-war in a fetid echo chamber resonating with shibboleths and platitudes. Canadians are even less aware that their hour has struck than they are of the prodigies of perseverance and ingenuity that brought them to this portentous opportunity. The bell of that opportunity tolls for us now, and the world, for once, will listen. It is our turn.

PART 3

PRESCRIPTIONS

1) Economics

Since there is an almost universal consensus that capitalism tempered by some level of social assistance to deal with the disadvantaged is the best method of economic governance in sophisticated countries, Canada should consider the two areas, the economy and the welfare apparatus, separately. The greatest engine of general prosperity is economic growth, and it should be encouraged. As President Reagan was essentially correct in saying that the only system of welfare that works is a job, job growth must be encouraged.

For most of its history, Canada was a branch-plant manufacturing country, a condition that has been somewhat mitigated by free trade with the United States, and a supplier of raw materials and agricultural products to the world. This was, until recently, something of the role of a hewer of wood and drawer of water, subject to the buffeting of international commodities markets. These were buyers' markets for raw-materials importers such as Japan, which could always invest in increased supply to keep a rod on the backs of the great Canadian mining and forest products companies and their analogues in other countries. But all this changed when China and India, representing nearly forty per cent of the world's population, ceased their vapid theorizing about economics, from Mao Tse-tung's Great Leap Forward and Cultural Revolution to Jawaharlal Nehru's pretentions to being the moral and political arbiter of the world because of India's acommercial and contemplative neutrality (as hundreds of millions of people writhed in desperate poverty in what Gandhi called "the ten thousand dung-heaps of India").

Now the suppliers have the better side of the market and demand is too great from the large developing countries to make it as hazardous to be in the resources sector as it was. Rather, manufacturing is constantly under pressure from more sophisticated labour-saving technology and from cheap-labour countries. The traditional problems of the economic cycle that led to tremendous spikes and desperate economic depressions have been smoothed by the systematic recourse to expansions of the money supply-inflation, sometimes moderately, sometimes not, but all currencies are declining in value and are measurable only against each other. If one consults the works of Dr. Johnson and Charles Dickens, a century apart, it is clear that the cost of basic goods and services in England had not changed, though there had been great economic growth and Dickens is best remembered for his portrayals of the less bucolic and less wholesome aspects of the Industrial Revolution.

After the Great War and into the Great Depression all the world's advanced countries chose to simply print money and spread it around in one way and another to alleviate the bone-cracking misery of hard economic policy. The

Keynesian theory was that in hard times, deficit spending was justified, and in prosperous times, surpluses could be run to retire the deficit. (This theory was hardly confined to Keynes but, like his contemporary Sigmund Freud, he gets the credit for many things which were as much authored by others, such as U.S. central banker Marriner Eccles, chairman of the Federal Reserve from 1934 to 1948.) Keynes also thought that there was "a natural balance" between spending, taxing, and minimal unemployment that would avoid inflation. This was rubbish, at least in practice, and Canada's achievement in balancing its federal budget fourteen years in a row was unique among large advanced economies in recent decades.

Anyone who has been a consumer for over ten years can see how vastly the cost of most desirable goods and services has considerably exceeded the official rate of inflation, and this is not a response to insufficient supply or improved quality of what is purchased, but mainly of a money supply increased to try to raise up the uncompetitive people in society. The motives are probably benign but are not disinterested; most of it has something to do with the attempted acquisition of political popularity and of statistical economic success. These are not unreasonable motives but they have created a prosperity that is based on policies that consist in part on setting the economy on a greased slide to the destruction of the value of currency and, with it, of savings, which is ultimately an assault on traditional middle class domestic economics and psychology—an assault on the vital organs of every modern democracy.

There has been almost no creative thinking applied to national economic and monetary policy since the rise of the

supply-siders and monetarists and the discovery of the power
of tax reductions to pay for themselves, which started to take
hold with the Kennedy-Johnson tax cuts in the United States
in the mid-1960s but was really entrenched with the Reagan-
Thatcher tax cuts of the 1980s. Canada has even failed to
assimilate these truths, though it generally gets the message
eventually, as it soon, presumably, will again, that it is dangerous to have personal and income tax rates substantially
higher in most brackets than they are in the United States.
The only opportunity to escape the truthfulness of that fact
would have been to scrap free trade arrangements and try to
barricade ourselves back into our domestic market, a crack-
pot policy, in the avoidance of which we have now to deal
with the uncompetitive status of Canada for people able to
choose where to pay their taxes.

    We should, as a practical matter, remind ourselves that the
purpose of economic policy is to promote domestic wealth
creation, equitably distributed, and to make the country
stronger through general prosperity and the high morale that
results from that condition while being at the cutting edge
in industrial and financial innovation to maintain our competitive and natural advantages of wealth, education, and
access and proximity to the greatest markets. Everyone in
the world envies us our advantageous conditions. We must
demonstrate that they are right to do so.

2) Nation-Building Investments

Canada needs an integrated approach to the most ambitious
strategic initiatives, especially in sectoral and infrastructure

projects. The late Jim Coutts and I were the only people I was aware of who favoured the federal government's acquisition of Chrysler Corporation when it was in desperate need of assistance in 1979. I was as vocal as possible in advocating, in the crisis of 2008, a Canadian effort led on the private side by the very successful auto-parts manufacturer Frank Stronach to buy control of Chrysler, and then to buy into shared control of Fiat Chrysler, with the Agnelli family, whom I well knew, when their company, Fiat, bought control of Chrysler, and especially when it was operated by Canadian Sergio Marchionne.

Former Canadian resident Elon Musk, founder of the splendid Tesla electric car, would, I suspect, after his current persecution by the U.S. Securities and Exchange Commission, be interested in joining forces with us. If the Swedes and South Koreans, who never built a car until forty years ago, can do it, we can. It is impossible to be a serious power in the world without partial ownership of a viable automobile industry. Only the U.S., Japan, Germany, France, Italy, China, India, and South Korea are really proprietary automobile producers, though Sweden and the U.K. get honourable mentions. Others are branch-plant sites or imitative manufacturers or fabricators, like Mexico, Spain, Brazil, Thailand, Turkey, Russia, Iran, the Czech Republic, Indonesia, Slovakia, Poland, and South Africa. Really, the U.K. and Canada are branch-plant countries, though they are the eleventh- and thirteenth-largest automobile-producing countries in the world. (In 1970, the U.K.'s production was mainly British owned, and nearly twenty per cent larger in units produced than it is now. Canada's production has almost doubled in the same period.)

There should be a revival of the economic formula that
so assisted the growth of the country throughout its history:
the public-private sector cooperation of Jean Talon to found
Canadian industry and make New France self-sufficient; of
Simcoe, and a century later Laurier and Sifton in attracting
immigration and laying out new communities, Macdonald
and Cartier, Strathcona, and Mount Stephen with the CPR,
C.D. Howe with war production the St. Lawrence Seaway,
and the Trans-Canada Pipeline, and even Pierre Trudeau with
PetroCan. One need only see the inspiration of the Daniel-
Johnson Dam or the Prince Edward Island Causeway, to see
the opportunity this majestic country offers to pursue physical and social projects on the immense scale of the country to
serve it best and invigorate Canadian pride. When I was a child,
a whole movie theatre would cheer when it was announced
that Canada had won a bronze medal at the Olympics. We
must keep growing, in fact, in pride, but not in ego.

There are a number of other major projects that could be
accelerated if there were public-sector participation, if only
as guarantors to ensure that capital can be secured at optimal
rates. The most obvious immediate need is the Canada East
pipeline that should enhance the prosperity of the energy-
producing provinces, to end our insane and demeaning
dependence on foreign oil imports in Eastern Canada; create construction employment across the country; generate
new refining capacity in the East; and that can be built with
minimal risk and no actual, as opposed to wildly fiction-
alized, offence to authentic Indigenous historical sites. The
dithering and balking over the construction of pipelines to
eastern Canada and to the West to feed the Far east market, that would benefit the whole country and eliminate our

partial dependence on oil-exporting countries that Canada politically disapproves of, has been a pitiful fiasco of official insipidity.

All of the major Canadian cities are objectively pleasant urban environments with excellent cultural and recreational facilities and big-league teams, fine orchestras, and interesting museums. Most of them have considerable architectural interest. More uneven are public transit and facilitation of all-weather movement through core areas, especially for pedestrians. A public-works program based on improvement of the urban ecosphere and encouragement of exceptionally fine architecture and urban spaces, would if administered properly, sharply improve and make more internationally notable all the major urban centres of the country. The long-awaited Arctic harbour should finally be proceeded with, and on a larger scale than the Harper government forecast.

The transformation of Toronto from a legendarily boring and drab city into a steadily more interesting and spontaneous environment can be said to have begun with the new city hall, the plan of which was selected in 1959 and completed in 1965. The Canadian Museum for Human Rights has accomplished something similar for Winnipeg, and several museums have played a comparable role in the evolution of Ottawa from a tank-town into a plausible G7 capital. Urban monuments can be created overnight, such as the Eiffel Tower, and they generally require more imagination than money. Even if it were not recalling a horrible and shocking tragedy, New York's 9/11 Memorial & Museum park would be a splendid urban space. All manner of projects could be successfully undertaken as public-private-sector ventures, as were the very successful Roy Thomson Hall and the Four

Seasons Centre for the Performing Arts (Canada's first real opera house, 139 years after Confederation). Nothing will attract high-quality immigration from all over the world as successfully as cities renowned for aesthetic and practically pleasant and prosperous living, and we already have most of the ingredients in many cities. Canada already has the best airports of any country in the world and is relatively well endowed with highways. We could easily and usefully put a good many people to work and become a much-envied country for superior infrastructure, especially in comparison with the United States, always a touchy criterion for Canadians.

3) Monetary Policy and Banking

The sensible, radical, and imaginative course is for Canada to reinvent the hard currency that has not existed in the world since the demonetization of gold. Here I agree with John Maynard Keynes, who thought even in the 1930s that the gold standard was too narrow and manipulable a base for currency valuation. Canada should tie the value of its currency to a combination of the prices of gold, oil, and a consumer shopping basket in equal thirds.

At the same time, it should lower the irritating and excessive restraints on the flow of money. It is really no concern of ours how people made their money as long as they have not broken our laws. If they are proved by courts in countries where we respect the judicial system and which reciprocate in these matters with us, we can freeze or seize and return what is proven by a legitimate legal process to be ill-gotten gains, but this should not be done pre-emptively. The Know Your Client regulations governing banking transfers are unreasonably demanding and time-consuming and are motivated more by a compulsion to regulate than by any rational desire to make illegal conduct more difficult. Obviously, Canada should not incite or be a haven for criminals, but a strong currency and relatively simple deposit-taking system would attract astounding amounts of capital which could be recycled into Canada to the general benefit of Canadians.

Another tax reform at the central-banking level is to put in place stand-by tax adjustments on consumption and income to deal pre-emptively with inflation-related fears. The long-standing practice has been to increase interest rates steeply to discourage spending, reduce borrowing, and restrain the money supply. Any such policy inevitably leads to a bone-cracking recession in an explosion of non-performing debt and an orgy of government-bond issues at astronomical rates that take ten years to work through the system. Each one per cent increase in the interest rate adds half a per cent to inflation until the economy is strangled by borrowing costs, and crumples, requiring pump-priming to be revived. It is an exercise in recidivistic self-imposed futility.

I propose that when inflation looms, goods and services taxes on all but the absolute essentials of food, shelter, clothing, and transport be sharply increased at once, according to stand-by criteria, so that an extensive parliamentary debate is not necessary, and that at the same time all taxes be removed from the proceeds of saving. This policy might not entirely solve the problem, but it would put the brakes on generally, and would make an important move to stabilize and counter inflationary spending in a way that would still reward the far-sighted without killing the overextended out of hand, as if in a terminal character-building exercise, and the great majority of the sensible middle class that does not speculate or borrow much or overspend, would not suffer at all, as those long-suffering people do in any recession.

As part of the policy to encourage capital inflows and investment, Canada's federal government should invite a province to volunteer to remodel its securities regulation system to provide a simple regime for the punishment of fraud and misinformation and unfair and inequitable treatment of stakeholders, and apart from that to allow substantial liberality in the issuance, marketing, and trading of securities. If this was understood to be durable policy in this country whatever provinces that opted for this status would almost immediately become serious international financial centres, and not just, as Canadian stock exchanges have always been, non-essential eddies of local resource promotion and small-capital start-ups and the odd site of a great international and inter-listed company. Canada could easily surpass Singapore, Hong Kong, and any other centre—except New York and London and perhaps Tokyo and Shanghai—as a world leader in modern securities issuance and trading. (Calgary would be a brilliant centre for securities trading and international investment banking. Unlike Toronto, it has not engaged in self-strangulation with a sociopathic securities regulator.) This, too, would attract huge quantities of capital especially from jurisdictions prone to intermittent over-regulation, including China and the United States. If Canada wants to be big, all it has to do is think big, and stop being a witless mimic of New York. An added benefit would be the humbling of the Ontario Securities Commission, which periodically tries to shoulder aside the other provinces and become a national regulator, and has become a capricious and pestilential tumour on the entire Canadian securities industry, such, in its stunted condition, as it is.

4) Fiscal Policy

In general, governments should be responsible and try not to spend, and the Chrétien, Martin, and Harper governments were exemplary, if not slightly fetishistic, in this regard. The spending envelope can be expanded if the fiscal and related policies are growth-oriented but non-inflationary. Certain national goals, most notoriously wars in which the survival of the country's vital interests and independence are at stake, justify expansive spending, especially if economic growth is such that deficits do not add appreciably to public debt as a share of GDP.

Instead of a rigorous criterion of balancing the budget, Canada should define national goals with serious spending implications, term them out reasonably, and keep all income taxes to thirty-three per cent personal and twenty per cent corporate ceilings, and adjust the rate on non-essential spending adequate to provide a comfort level that the proportion of accumulated federal debt to GDP does not exceed two-thirds. Spending is good as long as it is affordable and useful. With a hard-backed currency and a firm policy of not allowing debt levels to get over our head as an economy (i.e., within the fifty-to-sixty-seven-per-cent zone as a percentage of GDP), there will be incentive for investment, productivity increases, little inflation, and a benign cycle.

There is no point to obsessing on the percentage of spending occupied by the public sector, as long as public-sector
spending is intelligent and not based on excessive taxation or
deficits. Because of Canada's large size and relatively sparse
population, it will always require a good deal of infrastructure and this will require the intermittent continuation of
the fruitful collaboration of the public and private sectors in
economic expansion and supporting activities, the tradition
that has been described above.

Canada spent the first half of the last fifty years piling up
large deficits transferring money through the equalization
and other federal programs from the wealthiest provinces to
the less-advantaged regions, but in fact mainly to Quebec, in
the higher interest of preventing a breakup of Confederation.
The strain on the country's treasury and financial condition
was substantial and the Canadian dollar bottomed out in the
late 1980s at about sixty-five cents, U.S.

For most of the succeeding period, as was mentioned
earlier in this essay, spending responsibilities were piled
onto the provinces without accompanying sources of tax
collection being vacated, and the federal government bal-
anced its budget, though the provincial and municipal
governments were seriously strained. The Justin Trudeau
government has racked up significant deficits for no appar-
ent purpose that justifies such deficits, and has simply been
wasteful.

Now a new administration in the United States has sharply
reduced taxes, largely deregulated business, and has generated a sharply growing economy at about three times the rate
of growth of the Canadian economy and thirteen times the
rate of the growth of the economy of the Eurozone despite

the formidable and smoothly purring German engine at the centre of it.

There is no evidence to this point that Canada, as it normally does, is benefitting from this powerful surge in the American economy to growth rates recently over four per cent. And there is no serious policy alternative for Canada than to cut income taxes and replace lost revenue from other sources. Certain hideously expensive nostrums, such as the subsidization of renewable energy and the virtual state of war against the petroleum and natural gas industries and methods of their transmission, are bound to aggravate public-sector spending imbalances, and require immediate surcease.

Practically the entire energy program of this government should be dismantled and reversed, not only because it is extremely expensive and harmful to the Canadian energy industry, but also because it is based altogether on suppositions about climate change and global temperature and human influence on those matters that are unproven, and because Canada's contribution to the world's carbon use is a fraction of one per cent of the world total.

Canada's fiscal condition is too precarious now, for such a rich country, and we must in all areas incentivize economic growth and discontinue absurd policies whose stupidity is compounded by the fact that they seek undesirable goals to spare us from gruesome fates that do not in fact threaten us. The course of the present government in fiscal policy and the most closely related policy areas is a disaster and the only suspense is over whether it will take just one term in office or two for the country to realize that. Nothing short of a radical change, of course, will reverse the present sluggishness of the Canadian economy.

5) Resources

Canada's entire economy prior to Macdonald's National Policy of 1878 was based on extractive industry: what came from the mines and forests and agriculture of the country. With Macdonald's tariffs and the promotion of domestic manufacturing, Canada developed a considerable capacity in secondary industry, though it was very largely branch plants of British and American parents, as were, indeed, many of the mining- and forest-products companies.

As large underdeveloped countries got on the up escalator of economic growth, especially China, eventually followed by India and many others (South Korea, Brazil, Indonesia, and even, up to a point, Vietnam and Pakistan), the demand for Canadian base and precious metals, energy and forest products rose, as the competition for the manufactures from them also rose, especially in cheap-labour countries.

Paradoxically, instead of playing to its strongest suit, Canada, bemused by faddish environmental trends, and taking leave of the complete insignificance of any Canadian contribution to world carbon emissions, which have been singled out as the chief source of anthropogenic climate change, has manacled its energy and forest products and some of its mining industries. This may not be economic suicide, but it is certainly self-flagellation. Canada's possibilities as a manufacturing country are limited. The United States is not going to allow us to swamp its markets, and only in niche areas do we have a realistic chance of seizing foreign markets. Like much of Western society, Canada has effectively looked down its nose at blue-collar industry and imagines that the entire country can make its way in white-collar service industries. This is the ultimate economic fool's paradise.

If we are all university lecturers, consultants, and computer programmers, we will starve and our society will collapse. The world is composed of countries that can perform those services for themselves. All that we have that the world needs are natural resources. More than forty per cent of the stock values on the Toronto Stock Exchange are extractive industries that operate in Canada. The banking cartel lives largely off the resources companies, which feed all heavy, and most light industry, and the legal and accounting and consulting professions live off the banks and their principal clients.

We need to increase production in almost all of these extractive industries, do the drilling and build the pipelines to get the one thing Canada brings to the world's party to that party, and align our public policy with our national prosperity and security. By all means, let us encourage manufacturing, and if we handle the extraction properly, the manufacturing and fabricating of our basic industries will grow with them. But we should stop pretending that we are bookish and kindly office denizens in clean white collars embarrassed by our primary industry but eminently capable of building our living standard by simply peddling what other countries can do for themselves, but supplemented by our deferential personalities and incandescent virtue.

There has never been any excuse for why Australians have a substantially higher standard of living than we do. There is no excuse but there is an explanation: they are not ashamed of their natural resources and export as much as they can from what they extract from the ground to their Asian neighbours. The crusade the Justin Trudeau government has conducted against the oil and gas industries is a disgrace and it must be reversed. We are making fools of ourselves, self-impoverished fools. It isn't even good environmental policy, and it is a complete failure as economics.

6) Tax Reform

The entire tax system is an outrage, especially as the federal sales tax enables the establishment of a much more productive and less onerous and easily collected tax regime. Brian Mulroney opened wide the opportunity to finance increased government spending while reducing income taxes when he set up the GST in 1988. Prime Minister Stephen Harper reduced HST (as GST had become) from seven to five per cent, accomplishing the unique achievement among large advanced economies of reducing a federal sales tax. His implied goal in doing so, apart from giving the country a break, was to try permanently to shrink the size of the public sector. This, too, was an admirable goal, and it has succeeded, to the extent that the Justin Trudeau government has not touched the HST, but the Harper strategy has not prevented the successor government from raising income taxes and running substantial deficits, far in excess of what was promised and with rather dreary forecasts of economic growth and of a distant return to federal budgetary surpluses.

The advantage of a federal goods-and-services tax is that the necessaries of life for people of inadequate and modest incomes can be exempted. Work clothes, children's clothing up to a certain price per article, all food bought in grocery outlets, heating costs for homes up to a modest threshold of market or rental cost, and other essentials are exempted, and the entire tax base is essentially voluntary spending. Those who wish to avoid the tax can do so by not consuming, which will mean that they are saving or investing their money, activities which generate ancillary income to the public treasury. The whole psychology of taxpaying and collecting becomes less adversarial and therefore tax revenue is easier and less expensive to collect. All research and practice indicates that this shift in the basis of tax-revenue generation does lead to higher government income. While the Harper antipathy to the growth of the public sector was well intended, it implied a demarcation between the public and private sectors that was in itself disadvantageous. Earlier in this essay we saw how Jean Talon, John Graves Simcoe, John A. Macdonald, Wilfrid Laurier and Clifford Sifton, C. D. Howe, and Pierre Trudeau made public sector investments in important areas where the private sector alone would have been inadequately capitalized and the public sector unacceptably inefficient.

With the reorganization and reform described above, Canada would have a top personal income tax rate of thirty-three per cent, and a top corporate rate of twenty per cent. I also suggest a poverty-reduction tax that will be described below. Incoming investments and savings would be broadly welcomed and securities markets would function more freely than others, and major international companies would be encouraged to inter-list on Canadian exchanges. As economic growth is accelerating in the United States, our trade arrangements with that country will settle on a fairly neutral reciprocal flow, but that leaves an enormous prospect for growth. Traditionally, when commodity competition for the fulfilment by exporters of American requirements becomes challenging, the Canadian currency is reduced slightly in value. In the future, under the proposals above, that will not be so easy given the stability it will have achieved by adopting a neutral standard (based on gold, oil, and consumer products) to assure its value.

7) Welfare

The whole interconnected areas of job creation, education, and welfare and anti-poverty programs should be attacked as one massive policy challenge and not in the traditional manner of throwing at them more money, more study, more administration, and more unjustified rhetorical bunk about Just and Great and New Societies. The direction the Justin Trudeau government appears to be going in: embracing the universal basic income, which will in practice only be paid to people who fall below a designated line of inadequate income, appears to be based on hoped-for bonanzas from taxation of the Internet-gambling and cannabis industries. (It doesn't seem so long ago that our governments were doing God's work as well as the work of the leftist agnostic advocates of the perfectibility of man by sheltering us all from the unspeakable evils of ready alcoholic drink, accessible gambling, and any mind- or mood-altering drugs.) The greatest influence on contemporary mores has been official incompetence, not any cultural trends.

The universal income approach that is tempting the present federal government is an extravagant emotional laxative. Very few, if any, current Canadian governments have any capacity to downsize the civil servants and most have signed collective agreements that make that prohibitively expensive, and with the assistance of our Charter of Rights–intoxicated courts, such employees have an entrenched constitutional right to strike. The universal minimum income would pander to the desire of a very large number of Canadians to believe that they are the world's most caring and sharing people and that, in the wave of a signing pen over the legislation, we become the first large country with a general economy (and not just a petro-state like Qatar or Norway or a tax-haven state like Luxembourg, Liechtenstein, or Monaco), to have, by its imagination and generosity, disposed of the primordial scourge and evil of poverty. Unfortunately, Canadians, starved for a sense of uniqueness which complements an unslakable thirst for recognition, for which a strained self-recognition is a poor dietary substitute, could be vulnerable to such a pitch.

Certainly, the planners of Liberal Party election strategy could be more than capable of trotting out such a mildewed chimera. If enacted, there would be minimal bureaucratic saving, and to the extent there was any, it would detract from the human services provided by the state welfare apparatus, which, inefficient and slothful and hidebound though it often is, at least includes a great many dedicated people who provide valuable personal contact, experience, advice, and encouragement for those in need of it. A straight cash dole larger than what is already available, would be no substitute for that. And the anticipated revenue sources will not pay the bills, which all experience indicates will hemorrhage uncontrollably.

It is a bad idea, and if the opposition prepares its position properly, it will not fly politically, especially if the provinces opposed to the lobotomously misconceived carbon tax are successful in their political and legal resistance to that tax. Before the government and the Supreme Court attempt a coup d'état against any official toleration of the concept of God, as prejudicial to the interests of non-believers, those inclined to pray should apply themselves fervently, buoyed by the undemonstrative goodwill of fiscally sane agnostics and anti-theists, to the avoidance of this gestating policy catastrophe of a guaranteed income. It looks like scientific progressivism, but it is a confidence trick that will earn, if tested, a stark F in poverty reduction, fiscal responsibility, and ultimately, political judgment.

What we should have is a variation on Milton Friedman's negative income tax as an income supplement for those with incomes inadequate to get them above the poverty threshold, combined with assistance in skills development to help them bootstrap themselves up to self-sufficiency. To return to Ronald Reagan, this is the only welfare system that works: an earned income is the only generally successful way to sustainable levels of self-esteem, other than in the case of heavily handicapped people (who, all political factions agree, must be given every possible assistance). People in genuine need should have their incomes topped up as they pursue programs to assist them in income-raising skills development, and as employers are incentivized to engage them (with safeguards against them gaming the system by laying off more highly-paid employees to make way for subsidized ones).

A second strong line of attack on poverty, and an original one, unlike the guaranteed annual income which was being kicked around by Red Tories Robert Stanfield and Dalton Camp fifty years ago (when it was a fairly novel idea; they eventually thought better of it), is a small and self-shrinking wealth tax. People of net worth exceeding $10 million (and some leeway would have to be allowed to value non-liquid assets fairly conservatively), would pay two per cent of that, $200,000 in this case, which would be credited against their regular income tax, to fund a project of authentic poverty reduction through employment or a program to assist the poor to become gainfully employable. The projects would be approved as genuine, as charities and foundations are, and the rate of tax would gradually escalate, to a maximum of five per cent, on an individual net worth of $250 million or more. The rate would decline in all brackets as the defined percentage of the population of poor people declined. In this way, the most commercially and financially astute people in society would have a vested interest in the elimination of poverty and the interests of the wealthiest and the poorest people in society would be exactly aligned.

This is a much more effective way of uniting society behind the goal of poverty reduction than an expanded and unconditional, impersonal and statistically based dole to the poor, while riveting heavy income taxes on the wealthy, who have the resources to make excessively confiscatory taxes increasingly difficult and expensive to collect, as well as to source part of their income abroad. As poverty, by pre-established definition, was reduced, tax holidays would kick in, as the tax rate on the wealthy declined, and there would be a double incentive for society's wealthiest people to produce an incentive-based tax and poverty-reduction program. It would soon become as prestigious and admired as philanthropic munificence is, and would have the additional benefit of reducing the friction between economic echelons of society.

The whole process of taking money from those who have earned it and transferring it to those who have not in exchange for their votes would be replaced by a variously incentivized system of joint self-help: the wealthy assist the poor to cease to be poor, and the poor respond to the opportunities afforded them which automatically reduces the surcharge on the rich, who would be benefitting already from reduced income tax rates and increased consumption taxes, which can be avoided by the frugal with no danger of being accused of evasion. This would be a much more efficient, productive, and self-strengthening tax system than the longstanding tug-of-war between the redistributors and the supply-side advocates of prosperity through economic growth, derided by its critics as "trickle-down economics." And this really would be original to Canada, not another copycat acceptance of what the Western liberal death-wish processes in other countries through the sausage factory of dumb, stale, and unworkable ideas.

8) Education

A third attack on income underachievement, and not just poverty, lies in the education system. The federal government should not grant a cent of education-related assistance to any province that does not make a series of profound reforms.

The state schools in almost every advanced Western society have been virtually destroyed and for decades we have been generating steadily less well-educated people at ever-increasing cost and inconvenience to the societies upon whom have been inflicted these avaricious and lazy legions of underachieving teachers. With a great many personal exceptions, who must be allowed to percolate to the top and be prized and rewarded and recognized professionally, our corps of teachers pushes out or down those who are imbued with genuine enthusiasm for their work and for those whose formation they are guiding. In one of the major Ontario school districts last year, the response of the teachers' unions to the fact that objective testing showed students were less well educated in those schools than they had been a decade before, was to abolish the tests.

This is one of the most implacable symptoms of a decaying society: the collapse into illiterate and arrogant know-nothingism of the state school system; and a steadily greater consecration of public resources to produce a steadily more impudent, undereducated, and proudly, even aggressively, uneducated youth. The entire rotten system must be torn apart, destroyed, and many of its personnel dismissed, and the whole system reconstructed on incentivized, goal-oriented, and well-motivated teaching. Only those who have some interest in actually helping launch young people into the world can be allowed to teach, even if classes become bigger. The good teachers must be better paid than the unionized yobs who barely go through the motions of teaching anything.

All teachers' unions must be decertified and any attempt at industrial action during the school year should bring down severe and inescapable penalties on the perpetrators. Unionization has converted teachers in the state school systems into an industrial trade union and not a learned profession. Now, in the same measure that they threaten to strike in the school year and act like rapacious unionists, they deny that their goal is to blackmail parents and school boards and hold schoolchildren to ransom. The right to strike cannot be tolerated anywhere in the public service, and particularly not in schools. All that is needed is for the public to give the school boards and teachers' unions a crack of the fiscal hickory stick, and the political leadership should be eager to encourage that. They are the parents' children and only they can act.

One of the great acts of statesmanship I have witnessed in education matters in Canada was when the Montreal Catholic School Commission (almost all the French and about a third of the English schools on Montreal Island), went on strike, illegally, in the middle of the 1967 school year. The government of Daniel Johnson ordered that all teachers return to work. If ninety-five per cent of teachers had not returned to work within forty-eight hours, those who had not, unless they had a professionally attested family or emergency reason for not doing so, would be fired for cause. The union's assets would be impounded and its leaders physically detained at the pleasure of the attorney general of Quebec. When asked what he would do to reopen the schools if the teachers stayed out, Johnson said that one solution could be to place an officer of the provincial police and a closed-circuit television screen in each class, and he (Johnson), and his vice premier and education minister, Jean-Jacques Bertrand, would conduct the classes and $500 million annually would be rebated to Quebecers. He was obviously not entirely serious, and the teachers' union caved anyway. (Teachers are not like hard-bitten coalminers or steelworkers and rarely have unlimited stomach for confrontation, even with unruly students, much less the government that pays them.)

Regular examinations should be conducted in all schools to judge the level of achievement of students in a way that cannot be rigged by the teachers, and successful teachers should be rewarded financially. They can have a professional-level salary if they deliver educated children and not just the product of twelve consecutive years in a day-care centre with a little voluntary instruction on the side. A modicum of corporal penalties can be reinstituted for grievous or repetitive cases and in the hands of the head of school only.

Subversive organizations such as the Ontario Institute for Studies in Education should be completely repurposed with staff who believe in education and not just in the propagation of leftist inertia and the deconstruction of every legitimate academic subject. Celebrated intellectual Jordan Peterson is absolutely correct when he says that no academic subject described as "studies" is a real scholastic subject and that Western society would be better off without most of its schools and universities. He is right but that incites an unnecessarily draconian remedy to our education problems, profound though they are.

Higher education must be reoriented to address real needs. Here, education and employment problems conjoin. Immense outlays of public- and private-sector resources are being deployed to assure that people stay in school and university as long as possible. The most improbable and threadbare disciplines are being stretched into university subjects. The whole effort is designed to keep as many people as possible out of the labour market, which is overflowing now, because of the sluggish Canadian economy (again barely one-half of the rate of GDP growth in Donald Trump's America), and the growing shortage of real jobs due to increased automation.

Virtually every town in Ontario now has some sort of institute of higher learning. The whole concept is nonsense. Most of these colleges should be redirected to become schools to teach whatever society is short of, from plumbers to doctors. The skilled trades are underpopulated, but they need more status. Some universities are offering a kaleidoscope of studies in subjects that cannot possibly sustain much employment. Most schools of anthropology, for example, should be universities of practical science or some such, and should produce more plumbers, electricians, carpenters, and other skills that are needed and are remunerative. The provincial ministers of education should be incentivized by Ottawa to judge where job growth is most needed and direct the trade schools and community colleges, renamed as universities, to cater to these needs: market education. Forty years ago, every university graduate in Ontario was assured of a job. That is not the case now, and the universities and the witless government policies that created and directed them are responsible.

9) Employment

This leads directly to employment policy. Instead of desperately, and at crushing expense, trying to retain as many young people as possible in the workforce, keeping them from floundering into unemployment, we should institute national service, which should be universal except for various legitimate deferments, such as bona fide higher education, medical problems, or family conditions. It should be served civilly or militarily, and if civil, need not be residential and can consist of acquiring authentic practical skills in construction, education, social or welfare work, and basic administration, including business administration.

We need at least 100,000 more people in the armed forces. Canada cannot be taken seriously with a minuscule air force, almost no ocean-worthy vessels, and an army of three brigades. We need at least two divisions, a hundred first-class fixed-wing aircraft, new equipment for every-one, especially helicopters, a navy of at least twenty serious vessels, including an aircraft carrier, and a heavy infusion of strength into the Canadian aerospace and shipbuild-ing industries into the bargain. The military could also be kitted out in far more attractive uniforms, by Canadian designers, and that would help instil greater pride in mili-tary service, which the distinguished military traditions of Canada certainly justify. One need only look at YouTube videos of Italian carabinieri, or crisply professional and styl-ishly clad contemporary Chinese female soldiers to see how easily the martial career, even if used chiefly for assisting in humanitarian disasters, could be made more attractive.

The large pool of civilian draftees could be assisted into adult education, as members of the armed forces are, and assisted in acquiring skills society needs. They could also, within reason, remain in this form of national service, living in their own homes where practical, for an extended time. This would be infinitely preferable to trying to promote the fraud that they are in "higher" education, or in simply con-signing them to the lumpen-unemployed. Service would be for six months but extendable if the service-member wished and had no employment alternative in place. The particular needs for reform of the medical and legal professions will be

addressed later, in the health care and legal reform sections
of this sequence.

Competitiveness will be encouraged by the policy that I
have previously sketched out, of avoiding excessive manning
levels and discouraging labour unrest. Employees' rights will
be comprehensively outlined and enforced, but not against
obsolescence. The goal will be extremely efficient industry,
and those who become unemployed will be well paid when
laid off and assured of a living wage at once in the government labour pool in which all those in civilian public service
who are physically and psychologically capable of working
would be gainfully employed. The extensive automated
records of the manpower service would match those not
otherwise employed to situations available, including in the
income-enhancement activities of the private sector among
those applying the wealth tax to the elimination, in perfect
tandem, of poverty and the wealth tax. People would not
be pressured to take jobs they did not like, but nor would
they be paid to do nothing when reasonable gainful employment was available. Considerable enterprise would have to
be shown by administrators to prevent bureaucratization,
and new and needless offenses to the free market.

10) Immigration

One of the keys to increasing Canadian prosperity and
reduced dependency on the vagaries of international export
markets is to increase immigration. This has long been sensibly based on the merit system and those admitted are
generally those judged most capable of succeeding here.

Canada has an altogether admirable and widely recognized record as one of the countries of the world best disposed to immigrants and most welcoming to them. Of course, that does not mean that the way of a newcomer from a completely foreign place is easy but, once admitted, most cultures with sizable numbers of people already settled here have cultural and community facilities available to make newcomers more welcome, and both major Canadian political parties deserve credit for this record. This entire effort should be accelerated.

The whole history of Canada has been in substantial measure a demographic war to avoid being completely overwhelmed by the immensity of the United States and its swiftly rising presence by all indices. When the United States proclaimed its independence, it had about twenty-five times as many people as the several scattered provinces that comprised what is now Canada. A little over a century later, with Confederation in 1867, the ratio had narrowed to about fourteen to one. As has been mentioned, it threatened to balloon upwards with the immense flows of immigration to the U.S. between the Civil War and World War I but the Laurier-Sifton policy held it to twelve or thirteen to one. It was about twelve to one at the start of World War II and has since narrowed to about 8.7 to one. It should narrow still more in the near future as Canada is expected to reach forty million people by around 2025.[2] Because we have a land border with only one country, from which large numbers of people do not habitually flee,

2 At the end of World War II, Canada had one-fifth of the population of the United Kingdom and a quarter of the population of France. By 2030, Canada should have two thirds of the population of the UK and 70 per cent of that of France.

we have not suffered as Western Europe and, to some extent, the United States have from the swarming arrival, with no formalities, of masses of people fleeing destitution or barbarity and not seeking official admission to a new country to which they will pledge to commit and assimilate and get on and become patriotic citizens. That process is more an occupation of territory by a migrant mass of desperate, unskilled people motivated almost exclusively by the crudest desire for survival and unleavened by any great sense of the grandeur and virtue of the place where they have fetched up.

The Americans got to the very edge of an almost terminal problem: everyone welcome with no formalities at all, even the recording of names; all welcome to vote and census-takers not even allowed to ask if they are citizens for the constitutionally assigned purpose of determining the distribution between the states of the numbers in each state's delegation to the House of Representatives and the Electoral College. When people pour into prosperous countries in these numbers with no screening process at all, it is inevitable that there will be a great many undesirables and terrible social and fiscal strains. Canada has a perfect and enviable opportunity to attract large numbers of people that we would be pleased to have here. The most easily assimilable of all is the traditional basis of immigration, Europeans, and there are undoubtedly a great many Eastern Europeans who would leap like gazelles at the opportunity to come here. So would even some Americans, substantial numbers of Latin Americans, and large numbers of East and South Asians and Africans and people from the Middle East.

The facts that require some distinction between these groups must be faced frankly. We cannot knowingly admit militant Islamists, and while it would be offensive to screen people seeking entry on their religious views, we have the right and duty to pose the question of whether those seeking to reside in this country are prepared to pledge obedience to its laws, and to demonstrate a fundamental respect for Canada and its Judeo-Christian traditions whether they share them or not, and also for the sensibilities of its citizens. Those who so pledge and then break that pledge grossly or repeatedly must be expelled. I am not referring to controversial opinions, which everyone is entitled to express. Violations justifying expulsion of conditional immigrants must be outrageous crimes or repeated gratuitous affronts to practically universal opinion on a scale that constitutes a public nuisance.

Of course, immigration is a sensitive subject as traditional forms of employment tend to become more scarce through automation and the call of cheap labour on other continents, or at least as distantly as Mexico. In this era of strenuous pursuit of economic growth by previously underdeveloped countries, there will be ample demand for manpower in primary industry in Canada, where there are limits to what automation can accomplish. Larger resource and service industries (by which I mean essential services such as logistics, not an infestation of superfluous and noisome consultants and lawyers), can be fairly assured.

Some manufacturing and fabrication, though not of the most labour-intensive kind, can be repatriated to economize on transport costs, and an accelerating population creates and expands its own market. Canada, broadly speaking, demonstrated that it could compete in free trade with the United States after 1988, and at time of writing the United

States is demonstrating that it can create manufacturing jobs, incentivize the patriation of overseas profits, and generate immense job creation without inflation. Canada does not have anything like the sociological problems of the United States, the consequences of large-scale slavery and the undocumented admission of many millions of unskilled Latin Americans. Given our advantages, and the only disadvantage compared to the United States being one of scale, Canada should do as well as the United States is doing at the time of writing.[3]

A measure that would quickly expand the population would be the absorption of parts of the West Indies. All of Britain's colonies in that area were offered to Canada at the end of World War I but Sir Robert Borden declined. Bahamas, Barbados, Antigua, and Bermuda, would all be nice additions and as long as there were some residential restraints, Canada could effectively patronize those islands rather than Florida and make the economic development of them a strong focus of its assistance program. Some distinct status might also be possible with Haiti, a very backward and troubled country but one we could help and make a special project of for la Francophonie, as it is already a significant contributor to such increases as there are in the French-speaking population of Quebec.

One of the problems of any new and underpopulated country is a straight question of scale and whether it has

---

3 As of the summer 2018, U.S. GDP is growing at a rate of 4.2 per cent, compared to Canada at 1.5 per cent and the Eurozone at 0.4 per cent. For 2018 US GDP growth will be about 3.5%.

enough people and a clear enough raison d'être to be a viable country. Singapore is small, and Monaco and Gibraltar and Malta are very small, but there is a rationale for all of them. Canada has come through chronic underpopulation, and has gone a very long way to establishing a distinct identity, and certainly has no wish to be subsumed into the United States, and not just for ancient reasons of affection for the British (and Canadian) Crown and French Canada's fear of acculturation by the immense English-speaking population around it. Canada has generally been a better-governed country than the United States since the late 1980s, and functions better as a society, and it has made nothing, even on a suitably reduced scale, like the horrible American blunders of the Iraq Wars, the housing bubble, the Great Recession, and the actions that led to the immense numbers of desperate refugees in the Middle East. The America of Norman Rockwell and Walt Disney exists, as the Canada of Jeanette MacDonald and Nelson Eddy in *Rose Marie* exists, but the strength and weakness of the United States are that it is a tough, Darwinian, social jungle–country. It has astonishing stories of success and pioneering daring and achievement in almost every field, but it also has countless millions of broken people living in hopeless drug-plagued urban rubble heaps as well. Canada lives, to use a football metaphor, between the thirty-yard lines, and remains with the challenge of making that story as interesting as it is desirable, as rewarding of attention as the great human drama produced by the triumphs and tragedies of its neighbour.

There are some things that a country of fifty or sixty million people can do that a country of thirty-six million people cannot. We are almost at the critical mass that can be, and historically has been, the launch point for a world-important nationality. Nations of forty million people have been unambiguously great at many times in the past and present, and Canada, if it takes the lead in creative government, will be among them. It will finally shake off the oppressive burdens of always being the doughty, well-behaved, large in landmass but small in population country that was seen and not heard and rewarded with the occasional pat on the head from its illustrious relatives, the perpetually gangly, well-behaved teenager among nations.

11) Health Care

The Canadian health-care system, despite widely cherished contrary views, is a shambles. Because Canada generally compares itself to the United States, as the only neighbour and the world's most prominent country, we assume that if we have something that appears to be superior to the corresponding American version, it is the best in the world. This is what has largely occurred with Canada's national health-care program, Medicare. (In the United States, Medicare is a health-care program that covers those above the age of sixty-five. Medicare here is the Canadian program that provides health care to the entire country.) Here again, Canada indulges in delusion.

The United States' patchwork of health-care plans is really based on the profusion of private plans that are provided by employers and associations and cover about seventy per cent of Americans. The great majority of these people have very satisfactory medical care at very reasonable, if any, direct cost to the beneficiaries or their families. The remaining thirty per cent of Americans, almost 100 million people, have a very uneven variety of health-care plans, or none at all, whether by choice or lack of means, but all Americans receive health care. Contrary to cherished myth on the Canadian left, American ambulance drivers do not ask accident victims and emergency cases for their credit cards before taking them to the hospital. All emergencies are treated and patients can only be released if they are in a stable and self-sustaining condition.

But catastrophic health problems can be financially ruinous to people and families in the under-covered thirty per cent and there are frequent heartbreaking cases of such financial destruction for this reason. There is a general consensus in the United States that this gap in health care must be addressed, but there is no consensus on how to do it, other than to avoid the Canadian example, which after a great deal of research by Americans is seen as permanently bankrupt, largely inadequate, bound to produce impossible waiting lists even for emergency treatment, and likely to drive many of the most talented doctors to other countries, especially the U.S. Probably 20,000 Canadian doctors now live and work in the United States. This is no place for traditional Canadian nose-in-the-air condescension toward the United States.

Canada's Medicare is founded on the principles of universality: no opting out, no private medicine. It is "free," or without user fees, to all taxpayers. It is a straitjacket for the professionals who, in exchange for having their receivables guaranteed by their provincial governments, are effectively civil servants. In the interests of assuring that everyone has access to medical care regardless of his or her means, we cap the incomes of the profession, bureaucratize the entire process, grow uncompetitive in the attraction or retention of doctors, have a doctor/patient numerical ratio that is excessive compared to that of all other advanced countries, and allow the federal government to dictate this uniformity despite the fact that it now pays only about twenty-five per cent of the countrywide cost of the program.

Canadians have with fervent unanimity chinned themselves on the theory that Canada is the world's leading country in public health care because they have bought the fiction that only the rich get the benefit of American medical care, which is generally conceded, at its top end, to be the best in the world. It is political suicide here to contemplate aloud substantial changes. Every inquiry, and the parlous condition of the system in many respects requires frequent public inquiries, calls for more money. Health care takes ten per cent of Canada's GDP, which is one per cent above the U.K. and one per cent below Germany, but low compared to the seventeen per cent of GDP taken by health care in the United States. The American numbers are so high because seventy per cent of Americans are insured by their employers or by associations where the costs are tax deductible and are thus spread around generally and are effectively absorbed in reduced federal tax income, but that number, if it were accounted for correctly, would be offset by income tax on doctors and their corporations and employees and by sales taxes in many cases. This is no apology for the American health-care system, which almost all Americans agree is inefficient and not equitable and too expensive; it is only to say that these things are not exactly as they seem.

What Canada needs is more doctors, to shorten waiting times, and to make the system more accessible to the excessive numbers of people who crowd the medical anterooms and testing centres. World Health Organization figures for doctors per thousand people may not be entirely reliable, and may not distinguish between more and less competent doctors, and the quality of other aspects of health care, but Canada, with 2.54 doctors per thousand, the U.S. with 2.57, Japan with 2.37 (though the Japanese live longer than North Americans, allegedly because of greater reliance on seafood in their diets), and the U.K. with 2.83 take up the rear of the advanced world. The leaders are Austria (5.23), Norway (4.39), Switzerland (4.25), Sweden and Germany (4.19), Spain (3.87), Australia (3.5), and France (3.24). Perversely, chronically misgoverned countries such as Argentina (3.9) and despotic or totalitarian countries such as North Korea (3.5), Russia (3.98), and Cuba (7.5) show well. Obviously, some of these numbers are anomalous but they demonstrate that we should not be comparing ourselves to our normal competitors, the United States and the United Kingdom, but by this measurement in which Canada trails almost all advanced countries. The immediate answer is more doctors and it is contrary to Canadian foreign development policy to try to lure doctors away from underdeveloped countries, though Cuba could certainly spare some. To attract doctors from prosperous European countries will be challenging. We have the facilities to graduate and retain more doctors and should do so.

To this end, we should lift the prohibition on private medicine at once, a nonsensical condition that puts us in the same category as Cuba and North Korea, totalitarian dictatorships it is very difficult and risky to flee. There should be a minimal user fee, to send elsewhere those who attend upon their doctors for social or hypochondriacal reasons (these people must be cared for but not by such highly trained and widely needed specialists). It is a straight case of permitting the profession to supply the wealthier elements of society directly and at negotiated rates, which would enable them to raise their incomes while requiring all practitioners to leave twenty per cent or more of their billed time to the national health-care system. At the same time, medical schools should be enlarged by direct government grants, and all graduates should, in their first year of practice, in the context of the national service mentioned above, be available for three months in emergency clinics or deployed as required by administrators of the most crowded hospitals. We should aim for a doctor-per-thousand-people ratio about equal to that of Germany and Sweden (4.2). This would raise our life expectancy and sharply improve public health services with a resulting positive impact on public morale. We would then, as we do not now, have something to congratulate ourselves about in comparison to the Americans and the British (who have almost as ludicrous and misplaced a reverence for their National Health Service as they do for the British Broadcasting Corporation).

Those who use private medicine would relieve the public health-care system of those costs, freeing up more doctors and resources for relatively disadvantaged people. Doctors could operate in both the private and public systems, and patrons of private medicine would be entitled to a partial reduction of taxable income for tax purposes. This reestablishment of a medical private sector could be expected to

stimulate medical research and, in and of itself, be a significant incentive to medical research.

There will also have to be an expansion of hospital facilities, especially sophisticated diagnostic and surgical facilities.
The mania with which almost all of Canada's provinces
engaged in tearing down or abandoning hospitals to save
money was certain to be a failure, and indeed it has been, as
huge sums are spent each year expanding surviving hospitals.
The way to design a medical-care plan that serves the population adequately is not to shrink it to what is mistakenly
judged to be affordable, even when it is certain to be inadequate to care for all those who will depend on it for their
lives and health. It is to ensure that it is commodious enough
for its tasks and to incentivize the graduation of an adequate
number of professionals to care for the scope of problems
that elemental demographic arithmetic assures will exist.
With the private sector paying for a fifth or more of the cost
of health care directly, the unbearable pressure that is now
on the health-care system (which is otherwise impossible to
control or restrain unless we intend to shrink the population
as Stalin did in 1930s Russia by starving millions of people
to death and "liquidating" hundreds of thousands of others),
would be reduced to manageable size.

12) Justice

The justice system is in a more parlous condition than the
health-care system, even if the consequences are rarely as
life-threatening. Here there is the opposite problem: there
are not too few lawyers but too many—because of the annual

hemorrhaging of thousands of new statutes and regulations that require interpretation and adjudication. Viewed
altogether, the legal profession is the perfect 360-degree
monopoly, a cartel of restricted entry where its members
in their legislative capacities enact the laws and regulations, in
their governmental administrative capacity impose them,
in their barristerial capacity argue them, and in their judicial
capacity judge the arguments that must, of necessity, arise
over them. It is, perhaps inadvertently, but indisputably, a
profoundly corrupt arrangement which is sheltered from
the obloquy it would normally attract by a dense, almost
gelatinous cloud of pious claptrap about the rule of law and
the existence of the legal apparatus as being all that raises us
above the level of the jungle.

Of course we must have laws, but none of the great law-
givers, from Moses, Hammurabi, and Justinian to James
Madison and Napoleon, ever intended for this process of
access to an equal law for all, fairly applied, to become a
series of high-speed dispensaries of laws and regulations in
every jurisdiction constraining subjects in every conceivable
aspect of their activities, and supported by sanctions that
would spawn illimitable masses of constabulary and petty
officials to administer and adjudicate. Civil law, while con-
fusing and often strangling, is generally nothing that money
cannot solve, with a permit or a fine or a settled lawsuit.
(Bribes are an alternative in many foreign jurisdictions, and
if present trends continue, they will become more frequent
here, but there is no need to deal with them now.)

Lawyers cannot be allowed to continue the abuses of self-
regulation or immunity from regulation that they enjoy now.
Committees, composed of non-lawyers, must be established

in each lawmaking and regulating legislature to oversee and work with the relevant section of the Bar and represent the public interest in the governance of the profession. Of course, the law is a learned profession and must be treated respectfully, but lawmakers' self-regulating initiatives frequently affect all of society and the representation society has in these proceedings is the merest tokenism. Prominent members of other fields of endeavour should have a mandate to assist the benchers and equivalent Bar officials in ensuring that the public is not needlessly put upon, without compromising the integrity of the profession itself.

Each jurisdiction must establish a permanent commission to assure the consolidation of relevant statutes and regulations and the steady assimilation of new orders and laws in a way that keeps the body of laws and regulations as uncontradictory, as unclogged with authoritarian redundancy, and generally as simple as possible. It will be an unending task of trying to assure as manageable as possible a mass of laws and rules, without depriving the law of its subtlety and without accidentally moving the law away from precedent. Courts of Chancery should be revived to deal with equitable disputes. This could be in two divisions, a small claims activity that would replicate television's Judge Judy, and a higher level by the quantum of money potentially involved, to deal with straight money claims. Appeal would be preserved into the court system.

It is the practice now for all large law firms to profess to have an arbitration or mediation division, especially in marriage cases, but this is essentially a pretended service, taking the name of an alternative to full legal process in order to protect the share of the legal cartel the firm possesses. Most of these arbiters are superannuated judges, and most of these were not very Solomonic jurists in their prime. It is just a distraction, like the traditional newspaper trying to use the Internet to entice viewers into the paper, still functioning by the process of newsprint converted into printed product and surface-delivered, as it has been for nearly two centuries. There should be state arbitration panels, as there are courts, but with streamlined rules of evidence, almost unrestricted access and in such numbers that the present dysfunctional costs and delays in litigation are radically mitigated.

The entire problem was greatly aggravated by the Charter of Rights and Freedoms, and this arose after the acerbic exchange between the then premier of Quebec, Daniel Johnson, and the then federal justice minister, Pierre E. Trudeau, at Mr. Pearson's last federal-provincial conference in February 1967. As was mentioned in the historical section of this essay, Trudeau, in magnificent Rousseauesque flourishes, proposed to replace the squalid bickering between politicians about the prerogatives of each legislative echelon with the entrenchment of the only rights that were really important: those of the citizen. It assisted splendidly in taking the wind out of the sails of the Quebec separatists, but it invited every judge in Canada to become a legislator in applying the judge's own interpretation, no matter how idiosyncratic, of the Charter of Rights to whatever legislation gave rise to the issue before the court. I was one of those who feared when the Constitution was patriated and the Charter proclaimed in 1982, that the provincial legislatures would abuse their right to vacate provisions of courts in matters of civil rights, as Quebec did in attacking bilingualism. Unfortunately, what we have had is the exact reverse, and the legislatures have sat as torpidly as suet puddings while judges have reapplied the laws and reduced them to the status of inconsequential debating societies. It is an intolerable condition for any self-respecting elected legislator. But it will also shortly become intolerable for any normally active adult member of the public as the country's laws and precedents will become a tenebrous thicket impenetrable even to brigades of highly paid counsel.

One of the most egregious recent examples of this was Saskatchewan Federation of Labour v. Saskatchewan (2015), Supreme Court of Canada, in which Justice Rosalie Abella wrote for the majority an almost unbelievable phantasmagoric rollout of the Charter of Rights reasoning in place of what the legislators had actually enacted. The majority decision held that the right of assembly confirmed in the Charter overrode the right of the government of Saskatchewan to declare essential services of the provincial government to be ineligible for strikes because of their constant importance. It was the most astounding concatenation of juridical non sequiturs, the summit of the career of Justice Abella (a friend of the author and a very fine person who has carried water on both shoulders for the Ontario Federation of Labour for over forty years and on this occasion purported to hand the right to shut down even the emergency services of Saskatchewan to the public services unions). I was not surprised at the decision, having known its chief author for some decades, but I was shocked that the Saskatchewan premier did not immediately invoke the notwithstanding clause and vacate this hare-brained decision. Practically every judge in Canada is now cock-a-hoop imposing his or her own idiosyncratic versions of legislation. Someone must lead, but the notwithstanding clause's hour of destiny has come. The legislators of Canada must charge from their fire halls and hose down this pandemic of rampant outlawry on the bench. The intention of the legislator, Pierre Trudeau, was not to reduce the lawmakers of the country to mute spectators while every hobby horse indulged by the job lot of our judges tramples under its thundering hooves any notion of responsible government, the rule of legislated law, the high court of parliament, or even judicious rationalism. Nothing was ever meant to be like this, and someone has to bell the judge—literally, like medieval lepers with bells on their heads to warn the unsuspecting of their approach.

Pierre Trudeau himself told me, nearly twenty years after the patriation of the Constitution and promulgation of the Charter, that he never intended any such disorderly rout as had already begun to tumble out of the many courts and jurisdictions in his last years. Some concept of the intention of the legislator, in this case Trudeau himself, must be preserved. Otherwise, our legislators are redundant, and the law is an unfolding mystery, where ignorance of it will indeed be a practical, if not an acceptable excuse for violating it.

Apart from a heavy application of the notwithstanding clause, there is a secret corrective to federal excess now sheltering in the rations cupboard as the last chance for a resurgent coherent role for the legislator. Canada requires other urgent reforms. In addition to putting a rod on the backs of the country's judges and working out in practice a modus operandi between judges and legislators that accepts the ability of the bench to innovate and update in accord with rational interpretations of the Charter, parliament must assert and reaffirm that the ultimate law-making authorities are the parliament and provincial legislatures of Canada. Only the minister of justice of Canada can take this initiative, preferably with provincial and all-party support, and very soon. Our entire legislative and judicial system is a Gordian knot with no Alexander the Great to rationalize it. Deferring to the unelected judges excuses the elected legislators from their responsibility, an evidently dangerous state of affairs. The recently retired chief justice of Canada, Beverley McLachlin, was long the cheerleader for increasing the insurgent chaos.

In addition to making justice less ceremonious and more accessible, affordable, and swift, through Chancery courts and systematic arbitration and mediation courts, "legicare" should be put in place for criminal and some civil defendants of modest means. The public defenders are less of a mockery than in the United States, where most of them are just Judas goats for the prosecutors and have no authority to enforce plea bargains made with prosecutors. But Canadian public defenders, while rarely simply corrupt, are also rarely overly competent on the civil side, almost never adequately paid, and are insufficiently numerous and resourced to enable them to mount a serious defence against the crown. Scandalous delays occur in which defendants are detained without bail for unconscionably long periods without trial. The public defender system must be staffed adequately to ensure that a proper defence is possible and that criminal defendants who are reasonably judged to be dangerous or flight risks if bailed are tried within a civilized delay.

Compared to social programs and education, it would not be costly to fund the public judicial system properly and this is the most fundamental right of all. If the other reforms mentioned here were properly enacted, including, particularly, statutory and regulatory consolidation, there would be enough underemployed lawyers to staff the increased capabilities for indigent or incapable criminal defendants, and in some cases, where litigious oppression was suspected, civil defendants also. Such initiatives would be closely watched elsewhere in the world and would generate extensive activism in corresponding areas in all advanced countries. Canada would have a much greater reason for national pride in such activities as these than it has for excessive complacency about its ability to keep the peace in strife-torn foreign countries.

Penal reform is also an urgent necessity and an area where Canada can easily lead the world forward. There is no excuse for imprisoning first-time non-violent offenders except in the most egregious cases, such as huge financial frauds. Large numbers of people, especially maladjusted Indigenous people and addicts, those looking at child pornography, and others with mental disorders are routinely sent to prison as a default, and they do not belong there. Obviously, Indigenous people who are prone to violence cannot be allowed to be a public danger any more than others with that condition can. But there should be special facilities for natives, as part of a complete reconstruction of our native affairs policy, which cannot be based, as the Justin Trudeau government's is, on treating every band and tribe in the country no matter how diminutive and indistinct, as an equivalent nation to the federal government. Those who look at child pornography may theoretically drive a market for it but as long as they do not spread it, sell it, profit from it, or disseminate it, they are not committing an offence. No one benefits from prison and only those from whom society needs physical protection should be quarantined there.

Psychiatric and behavioural therapy is necessary for some, and all who commit offences should be required to submit to therapy and skills training that will enable them to participate normally in life and should expiate their offences with contributed work and enforced austerity in living conditions, but not suppression of liberty and close confinement, unless they are repeat offenders. The great majority of incarcerated people are non-violent and imprisoning them accomplishes nothing useful and is only done because it has always been done. So was imprisonment for debt, until it wasn't.

The present nature of criminal treatment, worsened and made harsher and more gratuitously punitive in the Harper era, is stigmatizing, repressive, and designed to ensure the permanent alienation of convicted people, rather than measured punishment combined with provision of a useful and plausible alternative leading up the escalator to reintegration in normal society. The Harper government commissioned new and larger prisons as the crime rate was falling, on the theory of "Build and they will come, especially natives." It was, as opposition leader Michael Ignatieff said, "dumb on crime." Many prisons could be reconfigured and repurposed as assisted housing if their locations are not too remote.

Reform of the treatment of violent criminals is an area that must be approached with much-greater caution, given the risks involved with such people.

13) Culture

As has been mentioned, the lot of Canada in cultural matters has been difficult because it is only the third English-speaking country and the second French-speaking country, and it is extremely easy and attractive for talented English Canadians to be subsumed into the vastly larger and generally more tangibly rewarding film and literary world of the United States, and to some extent, of London and Paris also. But Canada is a much larger population than Britain was in the time of Shakespeare, and has a larger literate French population than France did in the time of Villon or Montaigne. We have to do everything we can to stimulate and incentivize a flourishing cultural scene in this country, starting with more money for film and television production, for authentic literary projects, and for enticing Canadian cultural fugitives back home.

Nothing encourages and reassures patriotic motivations and confidence so much as proud cultural leadership. Canada has got most of the way to a fully viable and internationally distinguished base of literature and painting and has some fine orchestras and good opera and ballet. We can build on this but cannot look with ghastly and earthy frugality and skepticism on this area. Cultural budgets do not immediately justify themselves, but it is a terribly important and rewarding field and we absolutely must accelerate growth in this area, as long as we are certain of seeding quality work and not just underwriting a narrow in-group of self-reinforcing mediocrity.

The National Film Board should be transformed into one of the great film-production houses of the world, and the CBC into two (one in each language) of the great broadcasters of the world. Canada has demonstrated that it can compete in many fields and has contributed or attracted many eminent figures in all these fields, such as Norman Jewison, Richard

Bradshaw, Northrop Frye, Étienne Gilson, Wilfrid Pelletier, Sir Ernest MacMillan, Glenn Gould, Margaret Atwood, Teresa Stratas, Marshall McLuhan, Alice Munro, and Jordan Peterson. This is an absolute imperative of becoming one of the world's great nations.

14) The Constitution: The Senate and The Court

This brings us to the noisome but necessary bramble of constitutional matters. It is one of the pleasures of nationhood, though a great deal of agitation often has to be endured to get there, for a nation to devise and reform its own institutions. Canada is a unique country, as the only transcontinental, bicultural parliamentary federation in the history of the world, and we have to complete the process of taking complete authorship of our federal structure of government. This would have the additional merit of knocking out the last underpinnings of the Quebec nationalists and other fissiparous groups that claim Canada is not a real country, but just a rickety, foreign-designed scaffolding put in place to frustrate whatever atomized group seeking autonomy enjoys the loyalty of the complainant.

The distribution of powers under Sections 91 and 92 of the British North America Act has not been much modified. It is perfectly in order, as has been the custom in the case of Quebec for more than fifty years, to conduct direct relations with foreign governments in areas of provincial jurisdiction, especially education, culture, and some aspects of trade and communications. The core of the 1867 arrangements, which have been continued despite much friction at times, are the traditional criteria of sovereignty: the federal government controls the currency and the money supply, national defence and the armed forces, sovereign foreign relations; taxes are divided in that the provinces have a concurrent right to collect direct (income) taxes. The provinces control education, and rights of property, and civil rights. This was the best that could be done in 1867 and the fact that it has been almost unchanged these 152 years, despite efforts by both echelons of government to alter it in their favour, indicates that it was a well-settled division of authority.

Some unfortunate consequences of this arrangement are relatively easy to fix, and can be managed almost unilaterally by the federal government. It is nonsense, outrageous, and a shameful thing that there are any trade barriers within the country, just as it is a disgrace that there is victorious opposition to the shipment of Western Canadian oil to Eastern Canada. All of this must cease. Supply marketing is a scandal which, at time of writing, threatens to split the federal Conservative Party, and was declaimed by President Trump after the Charlevoix G7 meeting. Canadians pay huge excesses in the price of dairy products to the benefit of a fairly small number of dairy farmers in Quebec and Ontario. If those provinces want to continue those arrangements, they can pay direct grants to the farmers, but not expect the whole country to overpay for these products. The Constitution must make Canada a common market. The federal government should give one year for the provinces to phase out what amount to internal domestic tariffs, even if grants within provinces replace them to some extent, and it should suspend all federal assistance to materially non-complying provinces after a year.

The principal bones of contention in the completion of the renovation of our institutions to reflect that Canada has greatly increased in standing since 1867 are to reorganize the Senate and Supreme Court to reflect a provincial co-interest in their composition and functions. In these 152 years Canada multiplied its population by twelve (where the other G7 countries' populations have also increased: tenfold in the United States and by from thirty to seventy per cent in France, Germany, Italy, Japan, and the U.K.), and has acceded to a level of international importance that the other six already possessed at or shortly after the time of the Confederation of Canada. All manner of alternatives for the composition of the Senate were bandied about in the harvest season of proposed constitutional change, the 1980s and early 1990s, before the advent of regimes in Ottawa that were so terrified of trying to resolve this thorny issue that it no longer dares speak its name in federal parliamentary circles. It looms yet as unfinished business.

Before discussing institutional reforms, it is always salutary to remind Canadians that our country is officially bicultural. There seems to have been a revival of the implicit theory that this is an English-speaking country and that French Canadians have the same rights as Portuguese or Chinese Canadians: full civil rights, of course, but no rights of cultural continuity with an official status, no right to participate fully in the life of Canada without speaking English. They have that right and those who would dispute them deserve and require a sharp rejoinder and a concise lesson from our history. The British army defeated the French army in Canada, very narrowly. The French Canadians were never defeated and particularly not by the English Canadians in the Seven

Years' War, when there were no English Canadians apart from a few thousand in Nova Scotia and Newfoundland (which did not join Canada until 1949). We should do ourselves the favour of recalling that the Canadians, French- and English-speaking, have never been defeated at any level above a local skirmish in Canada or on the battlefields of the world. This is a unique and remarkable record of both moral and martial success.

In this unique and brilliant martial history, the French Canadians have played an exemplary part which is little recognized in English-speaking Canada. English Canada remembers Quebec's absence of a desire to aid its mother country (oblivious to the fact that France put Quebec over the side in favour of Caribbean islands producing sugar and rum in 1763, and checked out of North America, taking everything but the copper roofs on the official buildings). The French regarded the Quebecois as illiterate yokels for two centuries until the astounding descent into their midst of General Charles de Gaulle in 1967.

English Canada has never known, as French Canada has for centuries, what it is to be alone, a small and not sovereign people, in the world. We must fill that vacuum with sincere national fraternalism, and stifle with education and moral reproach the tendency, too widespread even now, to dispar-age the French Canadians as shirkers and inferiors. By the pseudo-macho criterion of eagerness for combat, the French Canadians, in 1776 and 1812, were eager to defend the home country and were comparatively unenthused about fighting for the French and British in the First and Second World Wars, other than voluntarily where they were numerous and conspicuously good fighters. But they were much more ready than English Canadians to accept partial conscription to fight in Korea, where they had a more acute awareness of the danger of communism than did the English Canadians, who tended to see Korea as another American gig, though sponsored officially by the United Nations, of which Canada was rightfully proud to have been a co-founder five years before.

Although the demographic balance has shifted, and many more French Canadians speak English than English Canadians speak French, part of the composition of the Senate must respect the original covenant of the country's founders. The House of Commons will not easily concede authority to another governmental chamber, especially not an unelected one. But if the quality of senators is assured of being raised from the generally rather second-level group that it has long been, with exceptions (and not that that makes it a group inferior to the House of Commons, just a less electorally legitimate one), the Senate could be given more authority to initiate, delay, and provisionally amend bills, but it must always be possible for the House of Commons to overrule it eventually, even if after prolonged debate, and use of an exceptional voting formula (see below).

A second component of the Senate must be that it is partially elected, which will enable it to contend more credibly for an increased measure of authority. And a third component must, of course, be chosen by the provinces. I propose thirty senators selected by the federal government, of whom fifteen must be primarily English-speaking and fifteen must be primarily French-speaking; another thirty senators selected by the provincial governments or province-wide populations, appointed or elected as each province chooses; and thirty elected senators. Every province must be represented, which means that Prince Edward Island, which has less than one-thirtieth of the population of Canada, would have three senators, raising the number of senators to 93. Those who are legitimate claimants to being Indigenous elect three senators among people who are qualified by their genealogy. The provinces jointly name one Indigenous senator, alternating between the provinces that have a defined significant number of natives, and the federal government would also name one. Appointments should be for renewable five-year terms and senators should serve to any age as long as they undergo medical examinations each year after the age seventy-five to assure that they remain capable. There should be five vacancies at the start of each parliament, which the government may fill during that parliament and for the life of that parliament. And, to give the Senate more importance, talent, and cachet, where there is a division on a confidence issue in the House of Commons, those senators who are elected may vote in the House of Commons on that issue. The addition of their votes could delay for a year unless a compromise is reached in that time, the adoption of legislation, but it should not by the addition of these votes, cause the fall of a government that retains majority support in the House of Commons.

It should be binding on all nominees to the Senate, whether appointed or elected, to demonstrate to a specially created panel of the Elections Commission some level of expertise in a useful subject relevant to public policy and all provincial governments, and the federal government should be admonished in the Constitution to seek exceptionally talented and distinguished people as senators. Where the Elections Commission does not approve a proposed senator, the nominating jurisdiction may force the election by vote of its own parliament. This is somewhat like the British House of Lords, which is almost entirely composed of life peers, not hereditary peers: people from most of the principal universities, leading corporations, and unions, as well as eminent cultural and religious figures (such as P. D. James, Yehudi Menuhin, Andrew Lloyd Webber, Asa Briggs, Chief Rabbi Jonathan Sacks, and Robert Skidelsky), are, or were, there. It is the duty of all with standing to put forward or appoint senators to choose evidently talented people, especially those who will serve one term out of duty but do not wish for and would not accept a sinecure.

The Supreme Court should be selected on the basis of one Justice from the Atlantic provinces, two from Quebec, three from Ontario, two from the Prairie provinces, and one from British Columbia and the Territories. They should be named as vacancies occur, and the provinces should be involved, and the federal government should alternate in naming justices as the vacancies arise. In this case, a retirement age of seventy-five should only be waived one year at a time in individual cases and by act of parliament.

15) The Constitution: Head of State

It is antediluvian nonsense for Canada's chief of state to be a nonagenarian (or any) resident of the U.K. who comes to Canada every few years (and is an entirely admirable and distinguished person who in her reign of sixty-six years has never embarrassed any of her subjects once). And it is nonsense that the acting chief of state, in the absence of the monarch (which is ninety-five per cent of any year), is an appointee of the prime minister, approved by the House of Commons. "Governor general" is a colonial title and an absurd anachronism, and the whole idea of a stand-in for the monarch is preposterous. It was an immense controversy when the Pearson government endowed the country with a flag and a terribly complicated tangle of negotiations when Pierre Trudeau made Canada responsible for amending its own Constitution.

It should not be so difficult to craft a position of chief of state adapted to the people and country that Canada has become. Apart from its anomalous title and nature, the distinction of the holder of the office of governor general has declined in stages. The French had quite distinguished and even very distinguished governors—Champlain, Frontenac, de la Galissonière, the Vaudreuils, and others. The British had two stages: soldiers of varying quality from Carleton (Lord Dorchester), down to cranky Francophobes like Colborne and Craig, through able career men like Kempt, Bagot, Elgin and Monck (all excellent), to stable royals or intimates of the royals who were elegant and prestigious and took the job seriously, including Lorne, Connaught, and Athlone. The British finished with a field marshal and future earl, Alexander of Tunis, allied commander of the Italian theatre in World War II, and recalled from Canada to be Mr. Churchill's defence secretary. Canada started with very prominent people as governor general: Vincent Massey, General Georges Vanier, Roland Michener, Jules Léger, and Jeanne Sauvé; then tapered down to worthy but not exceptional politicians like Ed Schreyer; and the first ethnic choices, Ukrainian Canadian Ramon Hnatyshyn, the first Acadian, Romeo Leblanc, Chinese-Canadian former telecaster Adrienne Clarkson, Haitian Michaëlle Jean; and then earnest university administrator David Johnston, and now the peppy former astronaut Julie Payette, a good image for contemporary women but invisible after her first rather flippant comments about atheism, an inappropriate issue to be raised by someone supposed to be a unifying personality.

My suggestion is that simultaneously with proposing a tighter trading and foreign policy bloc of the more advanced Commonwealth countries: the U.K., Canada, Australia, New Zealand, and Singapore, which would have a combined GDP of about U.S. $6.5 trillion (exceeded only by the United States, the European Union, and China), we suggest that the monarch be joint chief of state with a president of Canada, which office would incorporate the position of governor general and be popularly elected for a five- or six-year term, renewable. This official would have augmented powers, somewhat like the president of France, and the prime minister would lead in parliament and chair the ministers of the various departments, as he/she does now. But the president would have the authority, as the French president has, to conduct foreign policy and champion other initiatives within the governmental structure, subject to parliamentary assent. Figurehead non-monarchical chiefs of state, as in Germany and Italy, are just stand-ins for deposed monarchs and are as devoid of authority as our governors general and theirs tend to be positions held by seasoned politicians kicked upstairs to this ceremonious and honorific position. I believe we need a resident chief of state with real powers, the retention of the monarchical presence, and the avoidance of the American method of complete separation of the legislative, executive, and judicial co-equal branches.

The position of lieutenant governor is completely redundant and antiquarian, though the occupants are usually people
of some distinction. The premier can sign bills adopted by the
provincial legislatures, and if there is a parliamentary crisis
within a province, the chief justice of the province can address
it, and if that person thinks it inappropriate to do so, or for
any reason declines to exercise that function, then the decision of whom to invite to form a provincial administration or
whether to call a provincial general election can be evoked to
the president of Canada. The lieutenant governor's ceremonial
functions (which are valuable) can be handled by a vice premier for the purpose or the secretary of state of the province.

Again, it is one of the interesting civic facts in having
a country at all to be able to devise and renovate national
governmental institutions. Some such system as has been
outlined here is far from lapidary but it would reflect a far-
flung Confederation, assure representative government,
preserve parliamentary traditions, and give the country a
properly functioning bicameral system blending popular
election with reward of personal distinction. We would avoid
the chaos of Australia's overly powerful Senate, and the rigid-
ity of America's co-equal branches where the executive and
legislature have no clear connection. This would endow the
Republic and Realm of Canada (or, true to Canada's tradition
of devising novel institutions for itself, the Royal Republic of
Canada (Napoleon claimed his 1815 empire was a republic)
with a resident and democratically chosen chief of state with
real executive powers but not to the point of being able to
ignore parliament in domestic, taxing, or extraordinary foreign policy matters. And Canada would retain an hereditary
co–chief of state of ceremonious function but maintaining

the monarchical tradition that has never been absent from Canada since the arrival of Jacques Cartier in 1534 (and that is still replicated in many of the Indigenous bands and tribes). These proposed reforms would amplify the uniqueness of Canadian federal institutions.

It will not be like falling off a log crafting a federalization of the Constitution that brings in Quebec without driving out others. But it can be done, unless, as has been the Harper–Justin Trudeau policy, the subject is ignored because it is difficult. Holders of great offices are not elected only to deal with what is easy. It cannot be approached again in eleven-sided negotiations, plus Indigenous people. None of the provinces will be more devolutional than Quebec, so what is tentatively accepted by Quebec should be generally acceptable to the others, and any note of decentralization conceded to them would be happily accepted by Quebec. In approaching this task, it should be borne in mind that sixty per cent of Quebecers would prefer, if it were available, the continuation of transfer payments and of avoidance of defence costs, Quebec controlling the money supply, at least in Quebec, while Quebec exchanged embassies with every country in the world. Harper and Trudeau have ignored the efforts of the Couillard government to resolve differences and sign on to the Constitution. Federalists will wait a long time for a Quebec government so amenable to avowed federalism.

16) Foreign Policy: The Inheritance

The foreign policy of Canada has developed and grown with an unbecoming languor and lack of imagination. As was mentioned above, it took from 1867 to 1879 to appoint a single diplomat—the high commissioner in London. The first was Sir Alexander Galt, a capable and accomplished railway builder and politician. It was another forty-seven years before a second embassy equivalent was opened in Washington. Vincent Massey was the first minister. The idea of a ministry in Washington had been proposed by Canada and eventually approved by the British in 1920 but it required another seven years to get the idea off the ground, although the British Embassy in Washington was by this time spending two-thirds of its time and efforts on Canadian matters. Two-term prime minister Sir Robert Borden was tempted by the offer of the post of British ambassador in Washington at the end of World War I, such was the pull of imperial solidarity in English Canada and the modesty of Canadian nationhood. Apart from a protocol with Japan in 1907 to admit a few hundred immigrants a year, the first foreign agreement that Canada negotiated as a sovereign state was the Halibut Treaty with the United States in 1923 (it was a considerable commerce). The department of External Affairs was only founded in 1923, with Oscar D. Skelton, who had favourably reviewed Mackenzie King's turgid book *Industry and Humanity*, as the deputy minister. Skelton hired all the founding members of the Canadian foreign service, with future prime minister Lester Pearson ultimately the most famous of them. At the start of the Second World War, Canada had only added two embassies: Paris and Tokyo.

There was no longer any need to cleave to England for fear of American annexationist temptations, as might have been the case as late as Theodore Roosevelt. And after World War I Canada had distinguished itself and was clearly no longer a colonial collaborator as it had been to a slight degree in the South African War, where 7,300 volunteers served. Borden was well regarded and participated successfully in the Paris Peace Conference deliberations and Canada emerged a founding member of the ill-starred League of Nations. The "Canadian speech" given annually at the League of Nations (referred to in the history section of this essay), the template for all future utterances of impenetrable Canadian smugness (and they have been very numerous and are still audible), was listened to with bemused impatience: "Canada lives in a fireproof house far from inflammable materials." Even by the platitudinous standards of these international forums, it was pretty tedious.

Such was the devastation of World War II, and such were the prodigies performed by Canada in the Allied cause—we had largely liberated Belgium and the Netherlands—that Canada's significance in the world rose markedly. At the end of the war, with France, Germany, Italy, and Japan largely devastated, and our former enemies completely occupied, Canada was vying with Gaullist liberated France as the third Western ally. It was not the least irony of his astonishing career that Mackenzie King effectively announced the opening of the Cold War after the defection of Igor Gouzenko, a cipher clerk in Ottawa, and the revelation of the extent of Soviet espionage activities. King and his chosen successors, Louis St. Laurent and Lester Pearson, were thus natural co-founders of the North Atlantic Treaty Organization, devised by the Americans, but composed initially of just twelve countries, of which only the U.S., the U.K., France, and possibly Italy, surpassed Canada as a military power. All three men arranged for Canada to provide export credits to the non-communist nations of Western Europe that had been ravaged by the war and as in so many other occasions, loyally emulated the United States' Marshall Plan, with correspondingly beneficial results. Canada had a good record as an alliance member through the Korean War and through the Suez Crisis (cursorily described earlier).

St. Laurent and Pearson lost the 1957 election and Canadian foreign policy under John Diefenbaker started off at an angle and then went so haywire within six years that it brought his government down. He began as a virulent critic of the St. Laurent–Pearson "betrayal" of the British, French, and Israelis, and spoke fervently about a Commonwealth trade bloc. This all proved to be hot air as most of Canada's GDP was either in the local branch plants of U.S. companies or in direct trade between Canada and the United States. By 1960, Diefenbaker, an ardent Baptist and a pacifist at heart who had not the remotest idea of the nature of Great Powers' relations and strategy, apart from being a fervent son of the British Empire wherever that led, was stirred by the allure of nuclear disarmament. Specifically, he decided that Canada should not fulfil its obligations to deploy nuclear warheads on the Bomarc anti-aircraft missiles which he had bought from the U.S., and practically shut down the Canadian aerospace industry when he cancelled the Avro Arrow jet fighter and the Orenda jet-engine program in 1959. The whole episode flagged Canada as an unserious country in foreign policy terms.

In office, Pearson was a more substantial and convivial player than the erratic and unworldly Diefenbaker, but still a boy scout among the Great Powers, if at least a rational one. He made a speech at Temple University in Philadelphia in 1965, in which he asked President Lyndon Johnson to cease bombing North Vietnam, just as the U.S. was ramping up its land participation in that war. There will always be argument about the strategic and international law justification for that escalation, but Pearson, who had been with the high commissioner in London and the minister in Washington before he was the external affairs minister, knew perfectly well that it was an outrageous breach of protocol to make such a speech and pandering to the incumbent president's domestic enemies while in the United States. North Vietnam was invading South Vietnam, a country the U.S. and its East Asian allies—Australia, Thailand, New Zealand, South Korea, and the Philippines—had pledged to defend and would all defending with combat forces. Intensive bombing of the North was central to any strategy that had any chance of success against the Communists.

Pearson was relying on the advice of his old External Affairs chum, Chester Ronning, an anti-American leftist and candidate of the CCF, who had been on the International Laos Commission more than a decade before and headed an unsuccessful peace mission to Hanoi in 1965. He was, to say the least, not an impartial observer, and knew nothing of warfare. The fact that the North ultimately prevailed does not mean that Ronning and Pearson were correct; the South Vietnamese defeated the North in the great Communist offensive of 1972, with no U.S. ground support but extensive air support. On this basis, peace was agreed in 1973 and domestic American considerations prevented the resumption of bombing when the North relaunched their invasion in late 1974. One may imagine what the Canadian reaction would have been if an American president had attacked Canadian foreign policy in a speech delivered in Canada.

Pearson followed this up by determining that Canada would no longer provide uranium for military use by other countries. It had done so for the United States and the United Kingdom, which now had thoroughly adequate stockpiles of uranium, and he had said before that he would do so for France also. He had known de Gaulle in London during the war and rightly esteemed his courage, intellect, and patriotic determination. How he could have imagined that such a shut-off of supply would not seriously annoy the French leader and have consequences in France's relations with Canada and Quebec escapes this writer's imagination. When I asked Mr. Pearson this, after he had retired from public life, he said that he thought de Gaulle would understand his point of view, as he was ceasing to sell uranium to any foreign country, and that he would buy uranium elsewhere. The last half of this surmise was correct. The visit of de Gaulle to Quebec in 1967, described above, was the country's first exposure to bare-knuckles interstate rivalry with a serious country and without the British and Americans to help us. It must be said that Pearson looked like a rubber-legged prize-fighter, but after a day of internecine debate, produced a reasonably forceful statement that gave de Gaulle the pretext he wanted to return to France without having to set foot in English Canada. (And despite his thunderous and eloquent incitement, he looked a little out-of-role as he mounted an Air Canada mobile stairway to his plane two days later.)

Trudeau, as part of his campaign to prove to Quebec nationalists that Canada was indeed an independent country and not, as they had long been in the habit of claiming, an Anglo-American puppet state, courted Third World leaders who were not especially sympathetic to the West, like Julius

Nyerere of Tanzania. He made a particular point of currying favour with Fidel Castro, who pulled out huge crowds to cheer him, and was ostentatiously deferential to the People's Republic of China before President Nixon opened American relations with that country in 1972. Trudeau professed to be a spheres-of-influence supporter, which was his reason for not stressing the widespread criticism of American policy in Indochina. But it also enabled him to join in the false claim that Roosevelt and Churchill had conceded Eastern Europe at the World War II summit conferences to Stalin and that Soviet domination of the so-called satellite countries was completely legitimate.[4]

The real game Trudeau was playing, like Willy Brandt and de Gaulle's immediate successors, Georges Pompidou and Valéry Giscard d'Estaing, was to agree that the superpowers were implicitly of equal strategic strength (though this was bunk, as President Reagan soon demonstrated), and to incite the belief in the press that if any of them visited Moscow or Washington or even made a tour of other important capitals like London, Rome, Beijing, or Tokyo, they had the

---

4 This is not the place for an extensive treatise on the Yalta myth, but at the Yalta conference in early 1945, Stalin did commit to the democratic rule and freedom of Poland and the other liberated countries. It pleased disgruntled British imperialists to blame the Americans for the Soviet occupation of Eastern Europe; disgruntled Republican office-seekers to blame Roosevelt, Truman, and General Marshall; Gaullists to blame the Anglo-Saxons as unreliable defenders of Europe (as if anyone else had liberated France); and neutralist professed members of the Western Alliance like Trudeau and West German leader Willy Brandt to accept Soviet domination of these countries, either with pleasure or with resignation, all for slightly different but complementary reasons.

ability to influence the delicate global balance of power at no expense of resources to their own countries. Trudeau fiercely opposed Reagan's Strategic Defense Initiative, a conventional, defensive, space-based anti-missile system, because it was "destabilizing," by which he meant that it might (and did) deprive him and others of the ability to pretend that they had more influence on the world than they did because of the supposedly razor-thin difference in the geopolitical strength of the USA and the USSR.

It was all an egocentric, self-important charade, and Trudeau felt very out of place in the new world of Margaret Thatcher and Ronald Reagan. He never had any understanding of U.S. politics, unlike Mackenzie King or Brian Mulroney, and on this one subject, like John Diefenbaker. Trudeau told me he could not understand why the Americans preferred Ronald Reagan to Jimmy Carter. Trudeau was quite cold-blooded in these matters. He did not object to Cuban airplanes (that were carrying soldiers to and from the supposedly civil war in Angola), landing in Newfoundland, and did not raise any protest at all when the Russians shot down a Korean airliner on September 1, 1983, on which eight Canadians perished.

He never raised a peep about the suppression of human rights in the Soviet Union, Cuba, or anywhere else, despite his incandescent solicitude for them in Canada. Intermittently, and especially in the last couple of years of his regime, Trudeau pushed for a third option for Canada and pursued a balancing of Canada's trade with Europe to offset its dependence on the American economic association. It was a fiasco. He offered his own arms control plan, based on "suffocation" of nuclear arms spending, and a disarmament conference among the nuclear powers, which he peddled to Romania, the East Germans, and similarly irrelevant regimes. Canada became a country with no power, hard or soft, buzzing distractingly around the capitals of strategically weak countries wasting everyone's time with sophomoric ideas. Trudeau had a brief infatuation with North-South: the northern and richer countries should join en masse in helping the poorer countries. His suppositions on energy use were rubbish. Nor could Trudeau resist the Club of Rome, which essentially held that economic growth was the problem, not the solution. It was all of a piece. Though he had a strong intellect, Trudeau had no original ideas. He was a worldly man but stuck in the backwater of French Quebec, peddling dated and hackneyed altruistic notions of how to address great problems. His foreign policy was a failure by normal criteria but was a success in its main purpose of obliterating the Quebec separatist case that Canada was not an independent country with a standing in the world.

This left a blank page for Brian Mulroney in 1984. He elaborated a foreign policy on the attempted acquisition of real influence for Canada, which he knew could not be done by courting the antagonists of the United States like Cuba and the Soviet Union. The only way for a Canadian prime minister to be seriously influential was to enjoy the confidence of the president of the United States and for that fact to be known in the world. Even when he was not as intimate with the president as was implicitly pretended, as in the case of Mackenzie King, it was assumed that the Canadian leader counted in Washington, and in Brian Mulroney's case it was true. He was very highly liked and regarded by Reagan and George H. W. Bush, as indicated when he and Margaret

Thatcher were the only foreigners ever asked to give eulogies at the state funeral of a U.S. president, Ronald Reagan, in 2004, (and Mulroney did so again, for George H.W. Bush in 2018). Mulroney got on very well with Thatcher and with West German chancellor Helmut Kohl, and helped turn an open-skies meeting (originally the idea of President Eisenhower, unveiled at the Geneva summit conference in 1955 and rejected by the Russians for thirty-five years), into a discussion of and agreement on the reunification of Germany, in Ottawa in 1991. This was the fourth and, to date, the last occasion when Canadian diplomacy had an impact on the course of world affairs involving the Great Powers (after King's message to Churchill concerted with Roosevelt in 1940, the Gouzenko affair, and Suez). Mulroney played an initiating and vital role in saving the lives of millions of Ethiopians in the great famine of 1984–85, and played a leading role in applying pressure on South Africa over its white-supremacist policy.

Mulroney's negotiation of free trade with the U.S. in the first Bush term, and solid support of the American-led alliance in the Gulf War demonstrated his solid reliability as an independent but loyal American ally. He was much criticized by the Canadian left as an American lapdog but this was nonsense, as he demonstrated by, *inter alia*, demurring from the American pressure on the Nicaraguan Sandinistas. Canada got full value for Brian Mulroney's famous talents as a negotiator, going back to his days as a Quebec labour lawyer. In sum, he had a fine foreign policy adapted perfectly and profitably for Canada, to the times and personalities. He was, by all normal criteria, the most successful architect of foreign policy Canada has had, rivaled only by Mackenzie King.

Jean Chrétien was not foreign-policy minded and did not really have a foreign policy apart from retrieving Trudeau's policy of deemphasizing defence spending and claiming to transfer defence resources to peacekeeping, building on the Pearsonian myth that Canada had some particular aptitude for and international standing to make peace between enemies, as if they were sorting out quarrels between schoolyard brawlers and not nations with almost irreconcilable conflicting strategic interests. He shrunk defence spending. He found it convenient to revive Trudeau's fatuous and degrading courtship of Castro. He was significantly absent from among the chief sympathizers of the U.S. after the terrorist attacks of 2001, though he certainly condemned them. He had nothing to do with the Iraq War of 2003, which proved a sage decision.

Paul Martin promised a full review of defence policy and greater independence from the U.S., which implied greater defence spending than the anemic levels it fell to under Chrétien, but he did not remain in office long enough to bring it about, though he did, inadvisedly, withdraw from continental air defence arrangements. Stephen Harper was indistinct in foreign policy matters, apart from his coolness to Washington, abrasions with the Russians, and emphatic support of Israel. His address to the Israeli Knesset in 2013 was one of the finest speeches ever delivered by a Canadian prime minister. Justin Trudeau has conducted an astonishing exercise in the attempted translation of Canadian political correctness into a soft power of self-celebrated virtue. It has not worked, other than, possibly—and this remains to be seen—in the eyes of the only audience that seems to matter to him, Canadians themselves.

The introduction of gender rights, right-to-work laws (which we should replicate rather than attack), and environment requirements into trade discussions with the United States, like hassling the Saudi Arabians and the Chinese over their civil rights records, has achieved nothing but economic loss to Canada. There appears to have been born, like a fungus in the minds of the Justin Trudeau government, the delusion that where other countries exercised an influence based on their economic or military strength, or very occasionally their cultural genius (ancient Athens), Canada could expect automatic deference to its own definition of civic and environmental virtue. It has been a ludicrous and increasingly embarrassing failure. Assumedly, Justin and his senior ministers and advisers will come to their senses before the economic cost and reputational damage of these nostrums becomes prohibitive.

This is all to say that Canada has never really had a strategically based foreign policy beyond supporting a principal ally, and we now have before us a splendid opportunity to create one.

17) Foreign Policy: The Institutions

Almost all important international organizations are in a state of sclerosis. The United Nations, NATO, the Commonwealth, and the World Bank are those most obviously and chronically in need of renovation, and Canada as a co-founder of all of them and a country that has incurred no real enmity in the world, is in a unique position to take the lead. We should start with our closest associations. The European

Parliament, with more translators than legislators, is not answerable to the governments of the principal countries. The European Union administration in Brussels constantly spews out authoritarian directives. Britain cannot abide such a regime. If Chancellor Merkel and President Macron force Brussels to accept the British government's terms, effectively a two-tier Europe with a common market and political integration only for those countries that wish it, Europe can be salvaged. Failing that, Britain is out, straight into free trade with the United States and Canada, and it is time to make an informal bloc of the U.K., Canada, Australia, New Zealand, and Singapore, with India as an associate member, as was suggested above; this would entail liberalized trade and as much political coordination as everyone is comfortable with, which would be far from stifling.

It would have to be called the League of Associated Peoples, or some such, to distinguish it from the larger Commonwealth. The British-resident monarch would be head of the league and of the Commonwealth and co-chief of the state of Canada, and this group, with 135 million people and over U.S. $6.5 trillion GDP, almost $9 trillion with India included, could make its way forward very satisfactorily between a renascent America; a muddled Britain-less Europe; a China deprived of the blank cheque accorded it by pre-Trump American administrations; and a Far Eastern zone led by Japan, South Korea, Indonesia, Vietnam, Thailand, Philippines, and possibly Taiwan (the last depending on how strained Sino-American relations become).

Canada should take the lead in rounding up all the countries in the United Nations that have an acceptable level of compliance with the Universal Declaration of Human Rights and give the others two years to reach that compliance level; those that do not would temporarily lose the right to vote, and have only observer and debating status. The Security Council should give a permanent vote to the U.S., China, the E.U., the League of Associated Peoples, India, and Japan, representing some of its friendly neighbours also: Russia, the Arab countries, the non-Arab Muslim countries, sub-Saharan Africa, and Latin America. Only the U.S., China, the E.U., the League, Russia, and the Japanese group would have, unto themselves, a binding veto; two of the others would be required to make a veto. The General Assembly votes should be attributed on a weighted basis, composed of equal components of population, GDP, and per capita GDP.

Obviously, China and Russia would veto all this, and the General Assembly would have to deal with an immense revolt of the despotisms and obscure and destitute countries for whom the United Nations has been primal scream therapy for decades. At this point, all those countries in favour could set up their own organization, meeting nearby but retaining their offices where they are until a reasonable compromise is reached, but withhold all contributions from the continuing United Nations until then. Some sort of compromise would be found without undue delay.

NATO should be expanded to include all passably demo-cratic countries in the world that seek admission: all member states guaranteed by all (with the understanding that there might be frontier adjustments in the case of Israel). World Defensive Alliance or something like that should be the new name ("North Atlantic" hardly applies to Italy, Greece, and Turkey, anyway—in international organizations as else-where, misnomers should be corrected eventually). Each state would commit, as a matter of continued membership, to maintaining a certain level of democratic functioning and of military expenditure, and to designate in advance a level of military force that would be available in the event of an unprovoked attack on a member state.

The "Alliance of the Willing" that NATO was allowed to become is a pusillanimous façade behind which everyone wants a U.S. military guaranty but won't pay anything for it. Canada should no more be a party to the continuation of such a pantomime horse as the United States should. This would be a mighty alliance that could deter any non-member from any illegal aggression; countries would strain to meet the criteria of admission and it would be a force for improved governance in the whole world. Australia, Brazil, Colombia, India, Indonesia, Japan, Mexico, Pakistan, all very important countries with a total of over 2.2 billion people, would be among the new charter recruits.

Detailed discussion of reforming the World Bank would mire us in the obscurities of development-based banking and would not be enlightening. Advocating the proposed radical U.N. and NATO makeovers would be enough of an international reform agenda to project Canada to the forefront of noticed and respected countries, provided it had the platform of fiscal and military strength and the credentials of an innovative legislative laboratory of reform that has been outlined, and was not just the recycler of withered truisms of the old soft left, tarted up with the trendy politically correct frippery that it is offering now.

18) Foreign Policy: The United States

Free trade has shown that Canada can compete with the United States, but there is no point seeking any more intimate relationship with that country for the reasons that have obtained since the time of Champlain: we would fold this country into that one and there is no reason or excuse to do that unless we give up hope of having a more comfortable country to live in, separate from but friendly with the U.S. Canada has clearly been better governed than the United States in the post-Reagan years, at least until the Trump-Trudeau years, and while it has been an aberrant time in America's national progress that at time of writing is being corrected in many practical terms, especially economic growth and foreign policy effectiveness, this is not being accomplished in a way that attracts Canadians. Donald Trump, will, I think, prove a very successful president, but anyone who imagines there are no significant differences between Canada and the United States should canvass Canadian reaction to Trump, albeit that Canada is spoon-fed the Trumphobic bile of the American national media traumatized and screaming at the demise of the political cartel that has so horribly mismanaged that great country for the twenty years that preceded and ultimately elevated Donald Trump.

To some extent, Canada faced a similar problem when Ronald Reagan was elected president of the United States. Pierre Trudeau confidently told a number of Canadian businesspeople, including me, that Reagan's tax cuts could not possibly achieve economic growth without prohibitive levels of inflation, which, of course, did not occur, as the United States created nearly twenty million net new jobs, even as

over forty million jobs were forfeited to cheap-labour countries or replaced by automation, and productivity sharply
increased even as the workforce grew. Justin Trudeau is
less economically literate than his father, but not apparently more evidently impressed by the virtues of economic
growth or the completely unique power of the United
States to generate astounding economic growth and spread
it around its population if the great American economic
engine is fed properly. Trump's America is, at time of writing (late 2018), and as has been mentioned, expanding at
twenty times the rate of the Eurozone and twice the rate of
Canada.

While Trump has not been an exceptional economic pio-
neer, as Reagan was in some ways, he has some of the Reagan
economic formula, and is a much more comprehensive revolutionary against the existing system. Reagan promised to
abolish three government departments and shrink government and did not do it. He is a great president because he
did produce an immense non-inflationary economic boom
after fifteen years of Vietnam, Watergate, dithering, and economic stagnation, and he won the Cold War. In this sense,
the arrival in the senior position in the Kremlin of Mikhail
Gorbachev was fortuitous and spared Reagan the custom-
ary problems of stagnation that usually attends presidents
in their second terms. (Roosevelt also was spared that by the
European and Far Eastern war emergencies and, of course, he
had and played the high card of running, for the first time in
the country's history, for a third and then a fourth term. Term
limits are all right conceptually, but on the one occasion in
American history when a third presidential term was sought,
the continuity of democratic civilization required that it be

won. There is nothing wrong with Canada keeping its leaders in place for over eight years, as it has done six times.)

The implementation of the proposals outlined here would narrow the population imbalance between the U.S. and Canada to about eight to one, or seven to one, if intimate arrangements were made with some of the Caribbean countries (though perhaps not the most challenging ones, Haiti and Jamaica). The ratio of the U.S. and Canadian economies would also be narrowed, and Canada's comparative hand would also be strengthened if the proposals for a league of Associated Peoples or some such mechanism were effected.

The steps proposed for the enhancement of Canada's cultural identity, and especially as an innovative laboratory of legislative innovation, would be noticed and publicized in the United States and the long era of Canada as an under-recognized but inoffensive handmaiden of mighty and benign but rather distracted America, would give way to a much higher American national interest in and regard for Canada than there has ever been before. Canadians would see and appreciate that the United States is not a bit as maliciously envious of other countries as most countries contemplating America have traditionally been about it. The Canada I have outlined would impress and gain the vocal esteem of America, which would not only be a welcome phenomenon in itself but would also cause Canadians to see themselves differently.

The United States could reasonably be expected to welcome the international initiatives proposed here, in respect of the United Nations and NATO. It would probably follow our move to a hard currency, and the whole correlation of intellectual and policy influence between the two countries would be radically improved from the Canadian perspective. It has evolved gradually and positively since the American Revolution, but Canada would achieve a sharp uptick with such a program as is outlined here.

The only policies we have had in the past that were successful with the United States were, successively, the determined autonomous country refusing to be consigned to an indistinguishable status with the British Empire (John A. Macdonald), the decent helpful neighbour, good and inoffensive and not very noteworthy (Borden and King in the 1920s; St. Laurent), the intimate ally joined at the ear to the man in the White House (King and Roosevelt and Truman, and Mulroney and Reagan and Bush Sr.). Diefenbaker and Pearson and Trudeau bungled relations with the United States and were not taken in the least seriously by the contemporary presidents—Eisenhower, Kennedy, Johnson, Nixon, Ford, and Reagan, although Trudeau and Carter got on well (but Carter was brusquely repudiated by his electorate). Chrétien and Harper were not friendly with Clinton or Bush Jr., yet Clinton rendered great help to Chrétien in dismissing separatism in an improvised, learned address on the value of confederations at Mont Tremblant in 1999, in the presence of the separatist Quebec premier, Lucien Bouchard.

When an American president is popular and prestigious in Canada, as Franklin D. Roosevelt was, it always helps the Canadian prime minister to be perceived as close to him, as with Mackenzie King, whose polls improved when, as in Kingston in 1938 and Ottawa in 1943, Roosevelt referred warmly to "my old friend Mackenzie King." When the American president is mistrusted in Canada, as Republican presidents (except for Eisenhower and to some degree George H. W. Bush) were, cordiality with them is a modest plus point. When the American presidents are regarded as nationalistic, as Nixon, Reagan, and Trump have been, it is not helpful politically in Canada to be friendly with them. In this sense, Chrétien and Harper were correct and Mulroney was not, but Mulroney had great influence in the world, by Canadian standards, because the world knew Reagan listened to Mulroney.

The sort of program outlined here would facilitate the Canadian leader always being friendly with the U.S. president because Canada would be seen as stronger than it has been in the past, more relevant as a political society, and more influential in the world. While being cordial with the United States, a prime minister would need to be neither the lapdog of the American leader, as Mulroney was falsely accused of being, or the flag-waving gamecock "standing up" to the United States in ways irritating to Americans and ineffectual at home (Diefenbaker and both Trudeaus). A Canada perceived to be strong and relevant and known approvingly in the world, and able to attract successful Canadian expatriates back to their home country, will make its way in the world and in Washington.

19) Foreign Policy: The Rest of the World

With the rest of the world, Canada will be of interest to the extent that it is a country whose public policy is interesting and worthy of emulation, is seen to be competitive and adding to its stature, is independent and sensible and a contributor of strength to NATO (or its successor), abetted by an increased military capability and alertness to strategic issues rather than the comparative passivity of the post-Mulroney years, and with a firm but conciliatory and influential role in broader international forums such as the United Nations. The key is to be seen as independent, a country whose support is potentially useful and worth recruiting, while retaining the King-Mulroney skill at persuading Americans along with the St. Laurent–Pearson skill at navigating between large and varied blocs of countries.

Nothing will assist our influence so much as a legitimate accretion of our economic, military, and moral strength and nothing will accentuate those clear facts as much as a suave and diligent pursuit of influence at the head-of-government level. This would require the companionability of Pearson and Mulroney, and in his strange way, King, with a level of economic and military force that is deployable and that Canada has not had before. Mulroney had great success and was much more appreciated in the world than at home for his actions to combat apartheid in South Africa and the famines in Ethiopia. But Harper was basically correct to emphasize Latin America over Africa in development aid and political coordination. Latin America is in our hemisphere and those countries are more advanced and accessible to us culturally and socially than all of Africa.

The political model outlined here could achieve prodigies of emulation in Africa, South Asia, Latin America, and parts of Australasia. Nothing succeeds like success and Canada, as all Canadians know, already contains important elements of British, American, and French institutions and attitudes. Adapted to the related but different people that we are, and the times we are in, our institutions and policies could be of great value to other countries, for emulation and adaptation. We would retain the benefit we have always had of not being a ravening Great Power trying to influence developing countries or supporting one or another faction within them. Canada's motives would not be suspect. Our goal is essentially an altruistic one, as we are not seeking influence for its own sake, and we only seek it to the extent that other countries have useful lessons to learn from the creative reform of a range of policy areas. Canada has never sought to influence anyone—it is only frustrated that it does not have much influence. In this sense, we are strivers as much as are the beneficiaries of our assistance. Others may benefit materially from our assistance, but we benefit from their approbation and respect in the enhanced recognition that we receive from them, and from the confirmation that we are appreciated and successful in the world: a great nation in our own right, at last. We began with the premise that Canadians are annoyed and unsatisfied that we do not receive enough recognition and attention in the world. The constructive redress of that problem is its own reward.

CONCLUSION:
GREATNESS AT LAST

This is the destiny, and the vocation, Canada could
have, not in the next century, but in the next five years
of imaginative government. For over four hundred years
Canada has toiled, in the shadows of its potential, and to a
grudging or indifferent recognition of a smaller status than
it has now achieved the ability to claim in the world. Since
Lincoln abolished slavery and restored the American Union
and let America be America, earning for himself the profound and permanent admiration of the whole world and of
all posterity, the United States has been the most prominent
of the world's nations. For a time one or two empires were
more powerful, but the United States, just eighty years after
winning its independence, was the premier country in the
world's imagination after a revolution, electrifying growth,
and an excruciating self-purification. There have been rivals,
some of them evil, some quite transitory, and America is
not excused from the duty of vigilance and the avoidance
of complacency and misgovernment, as recent decades have
shown. China approaches, the first Great Power to recycle
itself, and there are also on the scene fading nationalities

of the old world, rising nationalities, with changing groups and blocs, assembling and dissolving. But assertions that the United States is now a hegemon in decline are untrue on the visible facts.

Chipper, patient, and courteous, Canada has waited its turn, having tenaciously pursued an improbable destiny—a splendid nation in the northern section of the new world, a demi-continent of relatively good and ably self-governing people, engaged in the world, gamely, often admirably, and never discreditably. French and British and other Canadians have preserved the magic thread that has led from the time of Champlain through four hundred years to the present, connecting the Canada of ultimate flowering to its rugged and noble origins. And Canada kept pace in the shadow of America, which is why it remained in that shadow and did not fall behind. But after all the political disorientations, needless wars, economic disasters, and internecine strains in the post-Reagan years in the United States, Canada has come forward out of the shadow of America, if we can adjust to running without trainer wheels, and to lead more than we follow.

All Canadians, not least those so frustrated by the sluggishness of the country's progress at developing a vivid national personality that they contemplate seceding, sense an impatience that we are not moving fast enough and far enough up the ranks of the benign powers. It has never been a question of any form of aggression to propel us further or faster, only a desire for the world to see we govern well and that as we have learned from many other countries, we can teach them something, too. So we can. It isn't just peace, order, and good government, though that is a fine context, if unrevolutionary and neither dramatic nor heroic.

Our main chance is in advancing the art of government by applying some new techniques to a field worn down by the plough-horses of convention. The silent unhurried fruitfulness of Canada's experience is ready to produce for the world a new harvest of better government and a better society. We have no excuse not to be the best, and when we are, we will have no need, any more than we have the inclination, to boast about it. Mainly unspoken and with thoughts not fully formed, Canadians wonder, why not the best? Answer has come there, none; it is waiting, now impatiently, to happen.